beadstyle
fabulous chunky jewelry

Genevieve A. Sterbenz

CREATIVE
HOMEOWNER® Home Arts

CRE▲TIVE
HOMEOWNER®

A Division of Federal Marketing Corp.
Upper Saddle River, NJ

✱ BEAD STYLE is designed to make "hands-free" crafting possible. Stand up the book with the steps of the desired project facing you. Follow the steps as directed. When it comes time to go to the next page of directions, flip the page over, and the next steps will face you.

✱ Stand up the book and read here first.

✱ Then read here.

BEAD STYLE: FABULOUS CHUNKY JEWELRY

SENIOR EDITOR: Carol Endler Sterbenz
GRAPHIC DESIGNER: Kathryn Wityk
ASSISTANT EDITOR: Jennifer Calvert
PHOTO RESEARCHER: Robyn Poplasky
TECHNICAL EDITOR: Emily Harste
ASSISTANT DESIGNER: Stephanie Phelan
COVER DESIGN: Glee Barre
INDEXER: Schroeder Indexing Services
PRINCIPAL PHOTOGRAPHY: Steven Mays
INSTRUCTIONAL PHOTOGRAPHY: Dennis Johnson
CONTRIBUTING PHOTOGRAPHER: Damian Sandone

CREATIVE HOMEOWNER

PRESIDENT: Brian Toolan
VP/EDITORIAL DIRECTOR: Timothy O. Bakke
PRODUCTION MANAGER: Kimberly H. Vivas
ART DIRECTOR: David Geer
MANAGING EDITOR: Fran J. Donegan

Printed in China

Current Printing (last digit)
10 9 8 7 6 5 4 3 2 1

Bead Style: Fabulous Chunky Jewelry, First Edition
Library of Congress Control Number: 2006924702
ISBN-10: 1-58011-314-1
ISBN-13: 978-1-58011-314-4

CREATIVE HOMEOWNER®
A Division of Federal Marketing Corp.
24 Park Way
Upper Saddle River, NJ 07458
www.creativehomeowner.com

dedication

For my sweet friend and beautiful sister, Gabrielle

table of contents

introducing the collection

BEAD STYLE: Fabulous Chunky Jewelry is an imaginative collection of 50 bracelets, necklaces, and rings made in the chunky style using beads of every description.

Wildly popular, the "chunky" look features both high and funky styles that combine shapely beads in gorgeous colors to create a single-strand necklace, such as "Palm Beach" in turquoise blue and lime green, or a multi-strand necklace, "Lettuce Leaf," fashioned from chips of peridot.

There are bracelets such as "Paris Café," which is loaded with beads in blue, light pink, and raspberry as well as multicolored, eye-catching

| Wilma | Turquoise Desert | Gold Coast | Diamond Girl | Miss Priss |
| Pebble Beach | Raspberry Tart | Jagged Edge | Black Orchid | Jet Setter |

lampwork beads, and "Rock Candy," which is composed of several coils of memory wire strung with faceted pink crystals to form a sparkling cuff.

The collection also includes chunky cocktail rings such as the "Cosmopolitan," with its large sparkling pink rhinestone, and "Rock 'n' Blues," a great showpiece that features a highly polished, single turquoise stone.

Providing both inspiration and practical information, **BEAD STYLE** will show you exactly how to make each stunning piece. All the basics of making each piece in "The Collection" are illustrated and detailed in clear, concise, easy-to-follow directions and close-up photographs that reveal each technical aspect of the jewelry-making process. **BEAD STYLE** also includes "Beading Basics," a comprehensive minicourse in beading that explains the essentials of beading, from tools to professional techniques. Additionally, "Sources and Resources" provides an up-to-date, annotated list of places to buy the very best in jewelry-making materials and supplies. The work concludes with an extensive index.

| Melondrama | Rock Candy | Margarita | Love Knot | Confetti |

| Blue Velvet | Dalmation | Sea Glass | Silver Stream | Paris Café |

| Cosmopolitan | Wrap Star | Cherry Bomb | On the Rocks | In Bloom |

the variations

You will find that as you work on one design, you will be inspired to substitute different beads for the beads recommended in the directions. You may have an attractive stash of crystals that you are longing to use, or you may prefer a colorway different from that suggested. Or perhaps you prefer to approach a design using a technique with which you are more comfortable, knowing it will produce a piece of jewelry with a slightly different feel. All of the creative inclinations that occur to you while you are working are a natural and integral part of the beading process.

You will notice that as you leaf through **BEAD STYLE,** each of the

Palm Beach	**Limeade**	**Ivory Tower**	**Prep Time**	**Red Hots**

Spare Change	**Lettuce Leaf**	**Flat Rock**	**Provence**

chunky jewelry projects featured in "The Collection" has a "variation." I found that as I worked on a design, I began to think about interesting ways to make another version. In some cases, I changed the beads and the clasp; in other cases, I made a coordinating piece to complement the featured design. All of the projects featured in this illustrated glossary of variations were inspired by the featured originals.

No doubt, you will take off on your own creative path as you handle the beads, wrap the wire, or crimp the strands. The important thing to remember is that there are an infinite variety of ways to create a beautiful and chunky piece of jewelry. Be guided by your imagination and your personal style.

Crushed Ice	**Blue Rain**	**Sugar Cubes**	**Sunset**	**So Charming**
Ribbon Candy	**Orange Crush**	**Ocean**	**Souvenir**	**White Hail**
Manhattan	**Ice Cube**	**Fireworks**	**Trio**	**Rock 'N' Blues**

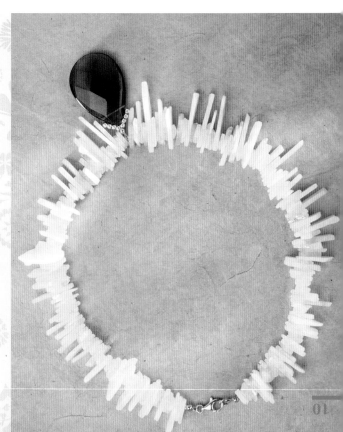

Wilma
Palm Beach
Turquoise Desert
Limeade
Gold Coast
Ivory Tower
Diamond Girl
Prep Time
Miss Priss
Red Hots
Pebble Beach
Spare Change
Raspberry Tart
Lettuce Leaf
Jagged Edge
Flat Rock
Black Orchid
Jet Setter
Provence

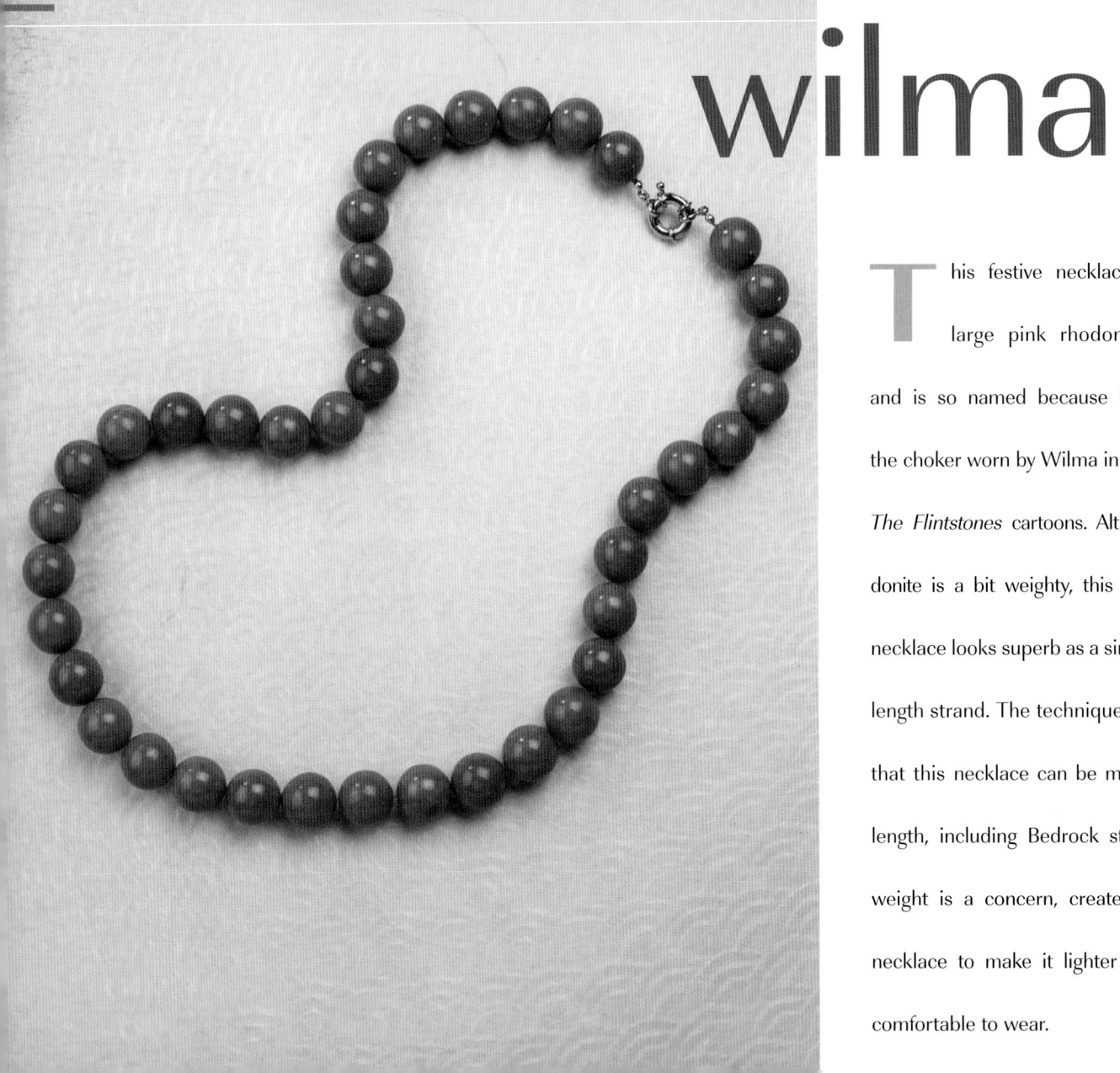

wilma

This festive necklace features large pink rhodonite beads and is so named because it suggests the choker worn by Wilma in the classic *The Flintstones* cartoons. Although rhodonite is a bit weighty, this substantial necklace looks superb as a single opera-length strand. The technique is so easy that this necklace can be made in any length, including Bedrock style! But if weight is a concern, create a shorter necklace to make it lighter and more comfortable to wear.

materials
- 38 round rhodonite beads, pink, 20mm dia.
- 2 crimp tubes, sterling silver, size 2
- 2 clamshells, sterling silver
- 1 spring ring, sterling silver, 18mm dia.
- 1 "figure 8" ring, sterling silver
- Monofilament, 30 lbs.

tools
- Ruler
- Wire cutters
- Chain-nose pliers
- Bent-nose pliers
- Crimping pliers

techniques
- "How to Use a Crimp Tube," see pg. 119
- "How to Use a Clamshell," see pg. 121
- "How to Use a Clamshell to Cover a Crimp Bead," see pg. 122
- "How to Attach a Clamshell," see pg. 121

Finished length: 30"

WILMA

1. Use the wire cutters to cut a 40-in. length of monofilament. Attach one end of the monofilament to the spring ring using a crimp tube and the crimping pliers. Then cover the crimp tube with a clamshell.

2. Use the chain-nose and bent-nose pliers to attach the clamshell to the spring ring.

The appeal of wearing this necklace is its elegant simplicity. Perfect for formal wear, "Wilma" can be worn anytime.

TIP
If the same bead is available in different sizes, create a symmetrical design with graduating-sized beads. Use the smallest beads at the ends of the strand and the largest ones in the middle. It's another great look and will cut down on some of the weight if the beads are heavy.

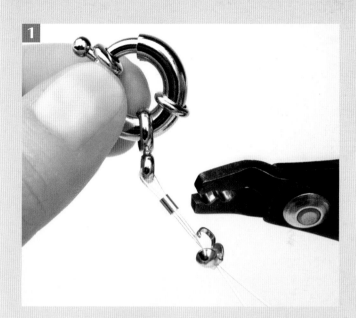

VARIATION: PALM BEACH

A lightweight, single-strand necklace with a tropical feel, "Palm Beach" alternates brightly-colored aqua blue and lime green beads. Further visual interest is created because the beads are different sizes. Because these glass beads are relatively small and light, they are a great choice for making a super-long necklace or when layering. Made the same way as "Wilma," this smart and easy-to-create necklace is finished with sterling silver jump rings and a spring ring.

Play out the hottest colors, like tangerine, pomagranate, deep red, and lime green. Mix the colors in a random design, or make several single-strand necklaces.

materials

- 29 round glass beads, aqua blue, 14mm dia.
- 30 round glass beads, lime green, 10mm dia.
- 2 crimp tubes, sterling silver, size 1
- 2 clamshells, sterling silver
- 2 jump rings, sterling silver, 16 gauge, 8mm dia.
- 1 spring ring, sterling silver, 7mm dia.
- Transite

Finished length: 28"

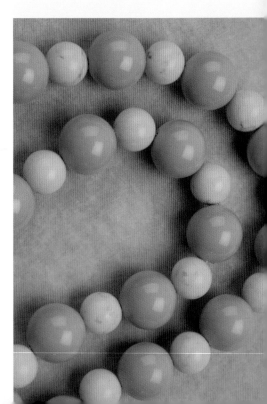

Certain necklace styles remain popular decade after decade, and this single-strand necklace is one of them. The "Wilma" design highlights the beauty of each perfect sphere. The rhodonite beads are a subtle rosey color that also have appealing heft.

WILMA

3. String one bead on to the monofilament, hiding the cut end of the monofilament in the bead. String on the remainder of the beads.

4. Use the crimping pliers, a crimp tube, and a clamshell to attach the "figure 8" ring to the end of the monofilament. Tuck the cut end of the monofilament into the last bead.

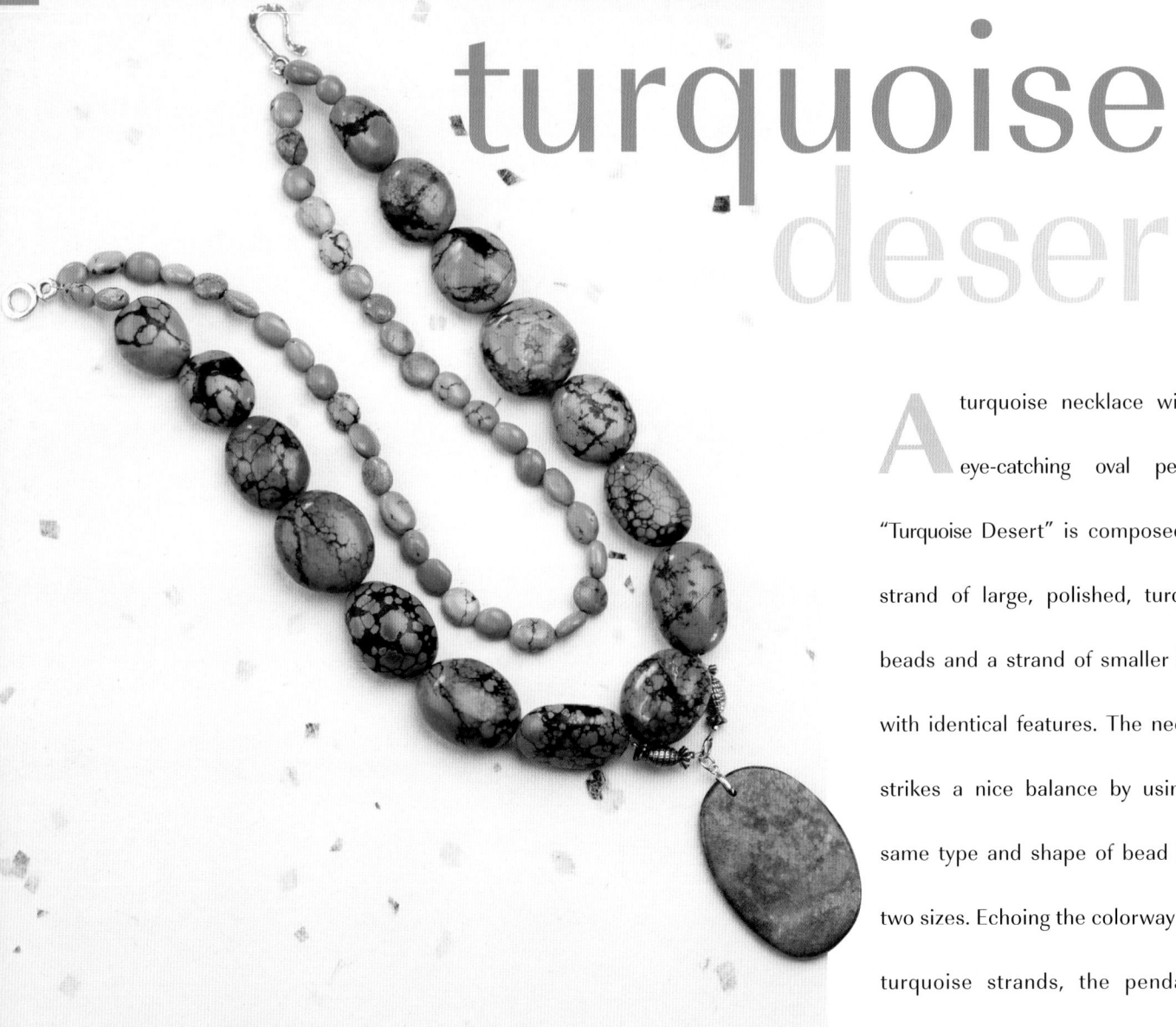

turquoise
desert

A turquoise necklace with an eye-catching oval pendant, "Turquoise Desert" is composed of a strand of large, polished, turquoise beads and a strand of smaller beads with identical features. The necklace strikes a nice balance by using the same type and shape of bead but in two sizes. Echoing the colorway of the turquoise strands, the pendant is attached with polished silver findings.

materials

- 1 flat oval turquoise pendant, 3.7cm wide x 5.3cm long x 4mm thick
- 15 oval turquoise beads, 2.5cm wide x 3cm long
- 40 oval turquoise beads, 8mm wide x 1cm long
- 2 oval beads, sterling silver, 6mm wide x 1cm long
- 2 discs, sterling silver, 6mm dia. x 3mm thick
- 8 crimp beads, sterling silver, size 1
- 1 jump ring, sterling silver, 16 gauge, 8mm dia.
- 1 hook-and-eye clasp, sterling silver
- 1 bail, sterling silver
- Beading wire, 0.40mm dia.

tools

- Ruler
- Wire cutters
- Crimping pliers
- Chain-nose pliers
- Bent-nose pliers

techniques

- "How to Use a Crimp Tube," see pg. 119
- "How to Open and Close a Jump Ring," see pg. 122

Finished length: 18"

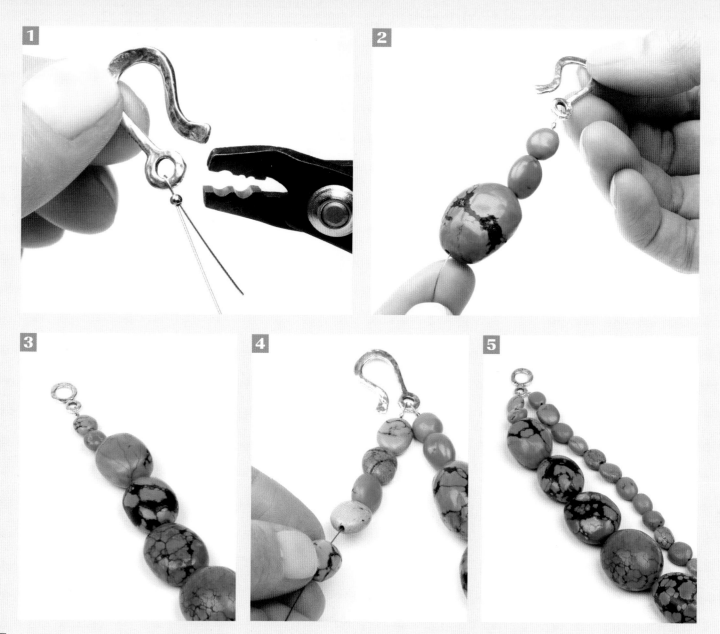

TURQUOISE DESERT

1. Use the wire cutters to cut two 22-in. lengths of beading wire. Set one aside. Use a crimp bead and the crimping pliers to attach the end of one length of beading wire to the hook portion of the clasp.

2. String on two small turquoise beads, 15 large turquoise beads, and two small turquoise beads.

3. Use a crimp bead and the crimping pliers to attach the end of the beading wire to the eye portion of the clasp.

4. Use a crimp bead and crimping pliers to attach the second length of beading wire to the left of the first strand on the hook portion of the clasp. String the remaining small turquoise beads onto the beading wire.

5. Use a crimp bead and the crimping pliers to attach the end of the beading wire to the right of the first strand on the eye portion of the clasp.

VARIATION: LIMEADE

This cool double-strand lime-green necklace with pendant is made using stabilized and dyed "turquoise" beads. The stones that make up the necklace are treated to a process that both colors and coats the raw material. The necklace features polished nuggets for the first strand and—for the second strand—polished round beads in varying shades of darker green that echo the matrix of the nuggets. "Limeade" is made using the same techniques as "Turquoise Desert." The first strand has six faceted lime-green beads at either side of the closure, while the rest of the strand boasts the nuggets. Round, polished beads make up the second strand. The necklace is finished with a sterling silver hook-and-eye clasp. To make the pendant, place a 3mm silver bead, one nugget, and a 2mm silver bead onto the head pin. Follow the directions for a wrapped wire loop to complete the pendant. Following the beading layout shown in the photograph at right, thread the beading wires with the remaining silver beads, and attach it to the nugget strand.

The classic shape and surface texture of real turquoise is expressed in an unexpected color in "Limeade" green!

materials

- 12 "turquoise" beads, lime green, 2.5cm wide x 3cm long
- 39 round "turquoise" beads, green, 10mm dia.
- 12 faceted round glass beads, lime green, 8mm dia.
- 2 oval beads, sterling silver, 6mm wide x 8mm long
- 9 round beads, sterling silver, 3mm dia.
- 1 round bead, sterling silver, 2mm dia.
- 1 head pin, sterling silver, 5cm long, 3mm head
- 1 hook-and-eye clasp, sterling silver
- Beading wire, 0.40mm dia.

tools
- Round-nose pliers

techniques
- "How to Make a Wrapped Wire Loop," see pg. 120

Finished length: 18"

TURQUOISE DESERT

6. Insert the ends of the bail into the holes in the pendant, and use the chain-nose pliers to squeeze the ends together.

7. Use the chain-nose and bent-nose pliers to attach a jump ring to the bail. Then cut two 6-in. lengths of beading wire, and set one aside. Use a crimp bead and the crimping pliers to attach one length of wire to the jump ring.

8. String on a silver disc, a silver oval bead, and a silver disc.

9. Use a crimp bead and the crimping pliers to attach the other end of the beading wire to the right of the center bead on the large bead strand.

10. Repeat steps 7–9 to string and attach a second silver beaded strand to the pendant and to the large bead strand.

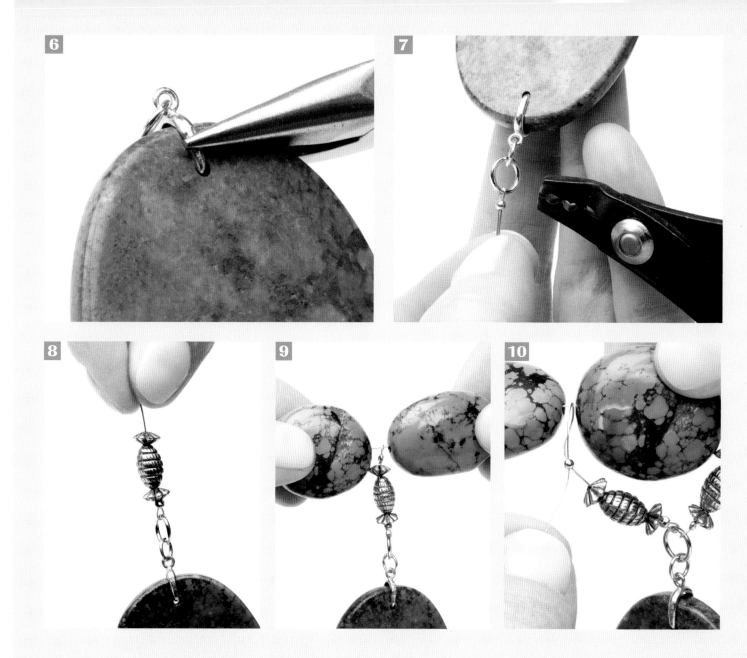

gold coast

L arge ribbed brass beads are combined with flat black discs and cream-colored beads to create "Gold Coast," a powerful fashion statement with African influences. Strands of black cord are used as a clasp and complement the design concept. "Gold Coast" is prominent enough to be worn alone, or it can be worn in combination with other beaded necklaces or gold chains.

materials
- 15 hollow brass beads, 3.5cm dia.
- 32 discs, black, 18mm dia. x 6mm thick
- 16 round beads, variegated cream, 10mm dia.
- 1½ yds. black cord
- 2 crimp tubes, gold, size 2
- Beading wire, 0.40 dia.

tools
- Ruler
- Scissors
- Wire cutters
- Crimping pliers
- Cyanoacrylate (instant glue) gel

techniques
- "How to Use a Crimp Tube," see pg. 119
- "How to Make a Single- and a Double-Overhand Knot," see pg. 121

Finished length: 34"

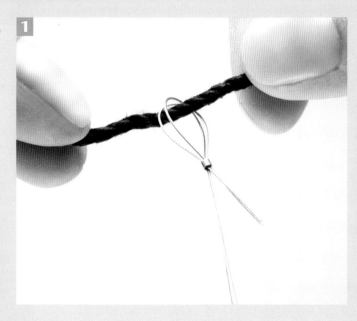

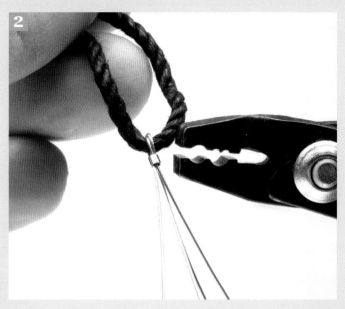

GOLD COAST

1. Cut two 24-in. lengths of black cord and two 38-in. lengths of beading wire. Holding the strands of beading wire together, attach them to the center of one length of black cord using a crimp tube.

2. Use the crimping pliers to secure the beading wire.

3. Refer to the photo on page 20 to string on the beads in the following sequence: a disc, a round bead, a disc, and a brass bead, repeating the sequence 15 times and ending with a disc, a round bead, and a disc. Thread the wire ends into the beads to conceal them.

4. Repeat steps 1–2 to attach the second piece of cord to the necklace. Tie a single-overhand knot at each end of the necklace, flush with the last bead.

VARIATION: IVORY TOWER

Carved ivory-colored bone beads alternate with shiny round red beads to form this exotic single-strand necklace. Like "Gold Coast," "Ivory Tower" employs a black cord as a clasp and is made the same way. It's a great "layering piece" and looks superb when combined with "Gold Coast."

materials

- 24 round beads, red, 14mm dia.
- 23 round carved-bone beads, ivory, 18mm dia.
- 2 crimp tubes, gold, size 2
- 1 yd. black cord
- Beading wire, 0.40 dia.

Finished length: 25"

TIP
When layering necklaces, combine ones that have distinctly different lengths and coordinating beads.

GOLD COAST

5. Add a drop of glue to secure the knot at each end of the necklace.

6. Tie two small single-overhand knots in all the cord ends, and secure each with a drop of glue.

TIP

The holes in the brass beads are large, and when they are used alone, a thicker stringing material, such as heavy black velvet cord, is required. Beading wire was used here because these beads are combined with discs and beads that have small holes.

diamond
girl

The focal point of this elegant single-strand necklace is a large rhinestone pendant, reminiscent of a snowflake, fashioned from a belt buckle. Large silvery pearls with silver endcaps; round silver beads, both large and small; and nuggets of frosted quartz crystal adorn the strand. This princess-length necklace sits high on the neck and features an intricate, symmetrical beading pattern.

materials

- 1 rhinestone belt buckle, 6cm dia.
- 9 glass pearls, silver, 14mm dia.
- 8 faceted frosted crystal nuggets, 1.5cm wide x 2cm long x 8mm thick
- 18 round beads, laser-finished sterling silver, 8mm dia.
- 4 round beads, laser-finished sterling silver, 6mm dia.
- 4 round beads, laser-finished sterling silver, 4mm dia.
- 18 bead caps, silver, 14mm dia.
- 2 crimp beads, silver, size 1
- 4 crimp tubes, silver, size 2
- 2 clamshells, sterling silver
- 1 lobster clasp, sterling silver, 12mm wide x 22mm long
- Ring portion of a toggle clasp, silver, 10 gauge, 14mm dia.
- Beading wire, 0.40mm dia.

tools

■ Ruler ■ Wire cutters ■ Crimping pliers ■ Chain-nose pliers

techniques

- "How to Use a Crimp Tube," see pg. 119
- "How to Use a Clamshell," see pg. 121
- "How to Use a Clamshell to Cover a Crimp Bead," pg. 122
- "How to Attach a Clamshell," see pg. 121

Finished length: 18"

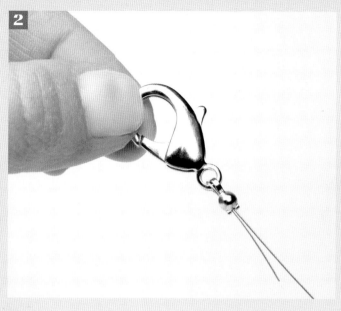

DIAMOND GIRL

1. Use wire cutters to cut one 22-in. length of beading wire. Attach one end of the wire to the lobster clasp using a size 1 crimp bead and crimping pliers.

2. Position a clamshell over the crimp bead, and close it to cover the bead. Then attach the clamshell to the lobster clasp.

3. Refer to the photo on page 24 to string on the beads, bead caps, and pearls. Hide the end of the wire inside the beads.

4. At the other end of the beading wire, attach the ring portion of the clasp using a size 1 crimp bead, clamshell, and the crimping pliers. Tuck the end of the wire inside the last beads.

materials

- 1 faceted quartz pendant, pink, 3cm wide x 4cm long x 1cm thick
- 5 fluorite rectangles, green, 14mm wide x 20mm long x 6mm thick
- 10 clear square beads with frosted edges and rounded corners, pink, 12mm wide x 14mm long x 3mm thick
- 6 clear quartz nuggets, 10mm wide x 14mm long x 8mm thick
- 13 iridescent faceted round beads, pink, 8mm dia.
- 22 faceted crystal rondelles, pink, 4mm dia. x 4mm long
- 4 crimp tubes, silver, size 1
- 2 clamshells, sterling silver
- 1 clasp, sterling silver, 10mm wide x 18mm long
- Transite

Finished length: 18"

VARIATION: PREP TIME

"Prep Time" is a play on "Preppie" because of this necklace's pink-and-green color scheme. This single-strand necklace combines translucent beads of different shapes and colors and is finished with a decorative sterling-silver clasp. The "crown jewel" is a large faceted pink quartz pendant. Follow the directions for "Diamond Girl." String on one each: round bead, nugget, round bead, square bead, rondelle, fluorite rectangle, rondelle, and square bead, five times. End with one each: round bead, nugget, and round bead. Cut a 12-in. length of transite for the pendant. Thread one rondelle onto the center. Thread both ends through the quartz pendant, a round bead, and a rondelle. Separate the ends and thread five rondelles onto each end. Use crimp tubes and the crimping pliers to attach the ends to either side of the center fluorite rectangle.

DIAMOND GIRL

5. Thread a 6-in. length of wire through a crimp tube, the right side of the belt buckle, and back through the tube; use the crimping pliers to attach the tube.

6. Thread on two 4mm round silver beads. Use a size 2 crimp tube and the crimping pliers to attach the wire to the right of the center pearl on the necklace. Tuck the wire end into the beads and trim the excess.

7. Repeat steps 5–6 with the remaining 6-in. length of beading wire on the left side.

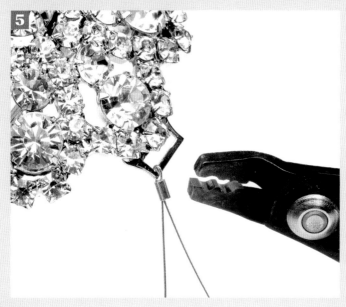

TIP
Rhinestones are a great addition to any necklace. Here, a belt buckle is used, but based on their construction, other options might include rhinestone brooches, pins, or earrings.

miss priss

Three graduating lengths of glass pearls in an antique cream tone make up "Miss Priss," an elegant necklace with ultra-feminine style. Small pearls are placed between the large ones to imitate the look of a hand-knotted necklace, a technique used to make real pearl necklaces. Instead of a traditional clasp, the strands of the necklace are secured at the back with a luxurious velvet ribbon tied into a bow with cascading streamers.

materials

- 170 glass pearls, cream, 8mm dia.
- 188 glass pearls, cream, 4mm dia.
- 2 clamshells, sterling silver
- 2 jump rings, sterling silver, 14 gauge, 16mm dia.
- ½ yd. double-sided velvet ribbon, black, ⅝" wide
- 1 spool of nylon beading thread, cream, size FF
- Masking tape
- Cyanoacrylate (instant glue) gel
- White craft glue

tools

- Ruler
- Scissors
- 3 twisted-wire beading needles for light-medium beading
- Chain-nose pliers
- Bent-nose pliers

techniques

- "How to Use a Clamshell," see pg. 121
- "How to Attach a Clamshell," see pg. 121
- "How to Open and Close a Jump Ring," see pg. 122
- "How to Make a Single- and Double-Overhand Knot," see pg. 124

Finished length: 32"

MISS PRISS

1. Cut three 40-in. lengths of beading thread. Thread each needle with a single length of thread.

2. Thread all three needles through one clamshell.

3. Pull the threads through the clamshell until the opposite ends are reached. Use a double-overhand knot to tie the ends together. If necessary, tie a second knot to ensure that the knot will not slip through the clamshell. Apply a drop of gel glue to the knot. Pull the knot into the clamshell, and trim the thread ends. Close the clamshell using the chain-nose pliers.

4. Set two of the threads aside. On the third strand, string three small pearls onto the thread. Then alternate large and small pearls.

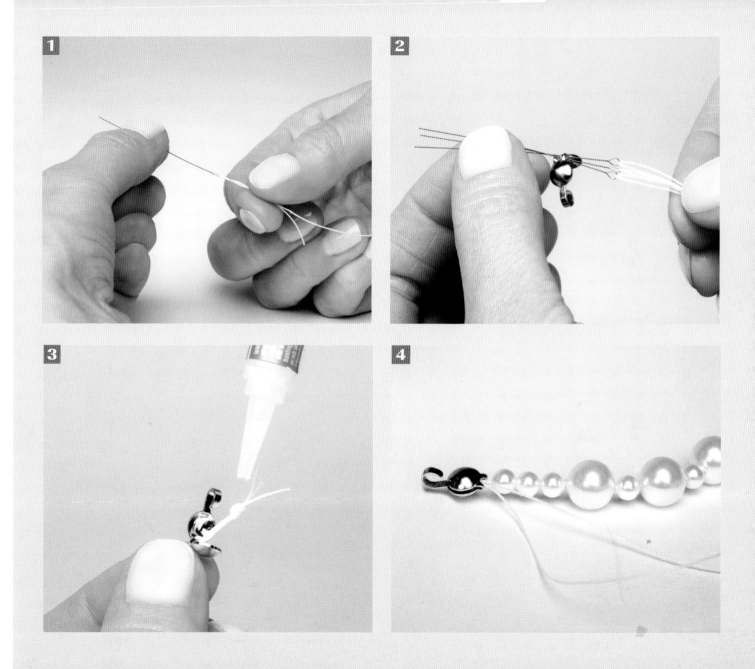

materials

- 118 round dyed jade beads, red, 10mm dia.
- 136 round dyed coral beads, salmon, 4mm dia.
- 2 clamshells, gold
- 2 jump rings, gold, 14 gauge, 16mm dia.
- ½ yd. grosgrain ribbon, orange with white polka dots, ⅝" wide
- 1 spool nylon beading thread, red, size FF
- Masking tape
- Cyanoacrylate (instant glue) gel
- White craft glue

Finished length: 24"

The small red beads make a delicate necklace. A slender ribbon adds a witty polka-dot pattern, echoing the coral spacer beads.

VARIATION: RED HOTS

This vibrant red-and-orange necklace with three graduating strands of beads features an alternating pattern of large red beads of dyed jade and small round orange beads made from salmon-colored dyed coral. Although the strands are shorter than "Miss Priss," this necklace is made in a similar way. The strands should be approximately 22¼ in., 20¼ in., and 18¼ in. before adding the last three beads. In keeping with the bright color scheme, a whimsical grosgrain ribbon in soft orange with white polka-dots is used for the bow.

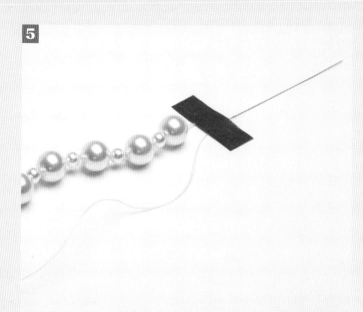

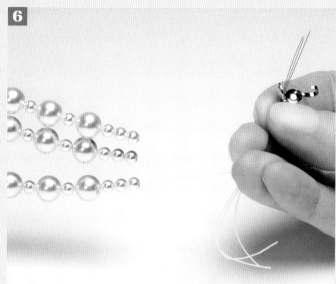

5. The strand should measure 30¼ in. and end with a large bead. (You'll string on three small pearls to finish the strand later.) Use a strip of masking tape to secure the strand to the work surface.

6. Repeat steps 4–5 for the remaining two strands. Measure the strands at approximately 24¼ in. and 22¼ in. before stringing three small pearls on all the strands. Thread all three needles through the remaining clamshell. Remove the needles, and repeat step 3 to secure the threads.

7. Attach the clamshells at each end to the jump rings.

8. Thread the velvet ribbon through the jump rings, and tie a bow. Trim the ribbon ends on an angle. Apply white craft glue to the ribbon edges to prevent fraying.

pebble beach

An elegant and sophisticated statement, "Pebble Beach" features a single strand of gold cable-link chain packed with small polished multi-colored stone nuggets in various shades. Each nugget and bead is fitted with a head pin that is wrapped into a loop, and then attached to the chain with a jump ring. This allows the stones to have a swinging movement when the necklace is worn.

materials
- 42" large cable-link chain, gold, 8-gauge, half-round wire, 7mm long
- 90 polished stone nuggets, various colors, 1cm wide x 1cm long to 2cm wide x 3.5cm long
- 5 clear oval cracked quartz beads, 2.3cm wide x 3.5cm long
- 95 head pins, gold, 22 gauge, 3cm long, 2mm head
- 95 jump rings, gold, 18 gauge, 6mm dia.

tools
- Memory wire cutters
- Wire cutters
- Chain-nose pliers
- Bent-nose pliers
- Round-nose pliers

techniques
- "How to Open and Close a Jump Ring," see pg. 122
- "How to Make a Wrapped Wire Loop," see pg. 120

Finished length: 40"

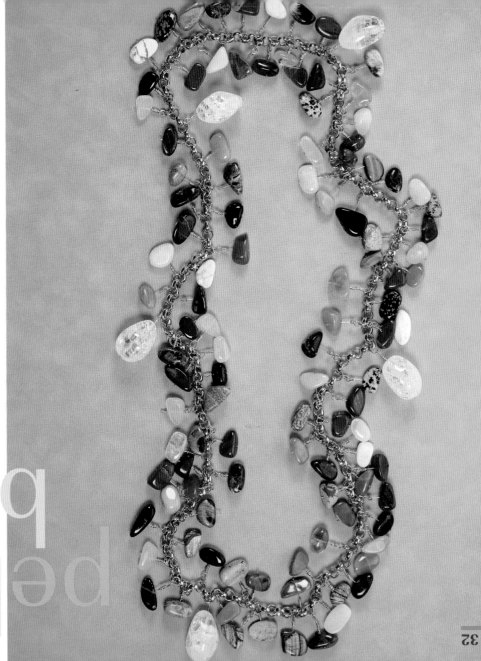

PEBBLE BEACH

1. Use the memory wire cutters to cut a 40-in. length of chain. Set it aside. Find the soldering point of an end link of the excess chain. Use the wire cutters to split the link open. Use the chain-nose pliers to open the link and remove it from the chain.

2. Bring the two ends of the 40-in. chain together. Thread the open link from step 1 through the end links to create a continuous strand.

3. Use the chain-nose pliers to close the link to create a continuous gold-link necklace.

The gleaming gold links that make up the long chain send off glints of light when the necklace is worn.

VARIATION: SPARE CHANGE

"Spare Change," an opera-length necklace, joins different styles of gold chain and is embellished with gold coins and bronze shell medallions. This necklace is constructed by connecting different lengths of chain using jump rings in two sizes, and only requires a few tools and techniques. Use the memory wire cutters to cut one each 20-in., 18-in., and 5-in. lengths from the 48-in. large-link chain. Use the chain-nose and bent-nose pliers to attach 3-cm, 14-mm, 3-cm, 14-mm, and 3-cm jump rings to both ends of the 20-in. length. Attach the 18-in. length to the last jump ring on one end, and the 5-in. length to the last jump ring on the other end. At the end of the 5-in. length, attach large and small jump rings in the pattern above. Attach the 18-in. length to the last jump ring to make a continuous strand. Cut a 20-in. length from the 24-in. small-link chain. Attach each end to the last 3-cm jump rings attached to the 20-in. large-link chain. Use the 5-mm jump rings to attach the gold coins and shell medallions in a random pattern on the bottom two-thirds of the necklace.

materials

- 48" flat chain link, gold, with alternating small and large circles, 10mm dia. and 14mm dia.
- 24" flat chain link, gold, with 8mm dia. circles
- 9 jump rings, gold, 10 gauge, 3cm dia.
- 6 jump rings, in gold, 14 gauge, 14mm dia.
- 17 jump rings, in gold, 14 gauge, 5mm dia.
- Gold coins:
  - 2 16mm dia. ▪ 4 22mm dia.
  - 1 25mm dia.
- Bronze shell medallions:
  - 2 12mm dia. ▪ 2 14mm dia.
  - 4 22mm dia. ▪ 2 25mm dia.

Finished length: 54"

TIP

"Spare Change" looks equally beautiful in silver! Different sizes and styles of chain and coins are available in both sterling silver and silver tone in jewelry-making supply stores.

PEBBLE BEACH

4. See "How to Make a Wrapped Wire Loop," pg. 120, for how to assemble the nuggets and beads onto head pins.

5. Create this necklace in three stages, attaching approximately 30 stones in each stage. Distribute the stones at random intervals, filling in spaces using stones in contrasting colors and shapes. See "beading stages layout" below for an overview of the stones' placement.

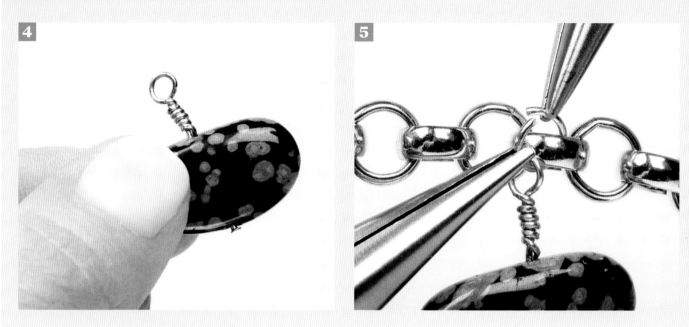

beading stages layout

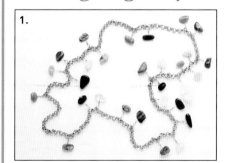

Stage 1.
Attach a jump ring to one stone and to the chain. Repeat to attach 29 more stones.

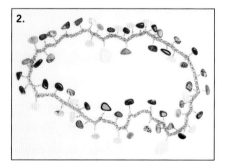

Stage 2.
Repeat step 1 to fill the spaces between the stones attached in step 1.

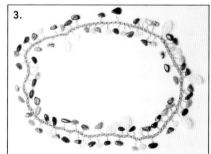

Stage 3.
Repeat step 1 to fill in the remaining spaces between the attached stones.

raspberry tart

The appeal of this sparkling necklace is the rich substance of the faceted quartz beads, in terms of their shape, weight, and dazzling berry-red color. Attached at the back with a gleaming gold ring clasp, this shimmering choker is composed of five strands of identical beads attached to golden end bars that separate the strands and keep them beautifully arranged around the neck.

materials
- 170 faceted round quartz beads, berry red, 10mm dia.
- 2 end bars, for 5 strands, gold, 3cm long
- 10 crimp tubes, gold, size 2
- 2 jump rings, gold, 16 gauge, 7mm dia.
- 1 "figure 8" ring, gold
- 1 spring ring, gold, 18mm dia.
- Beading wire, 0.40mm dia.

tools
- Ruler
- Wire cutters
- Crimping pliers
- Chain-nose pliers
- Bent-nose pliers

techniques
- "How to Use a Crimp Tube," see pg. 119
- "How to Open and Close a Jump Ring," see pg. 122

Finished length: 14"

RASPBERRY TART

1. Use the wire cutters to cut five 18-in. lengths of beading wire. Attach one strand of beading wire to an outside hole of the end bar using a crimp tube and crimping pliers.

2. Thread on 34 beads.

For a sparkling choker with more restrained color, string each strand with a mix of crystal beads in the very palest of tints like citrine, rose, lavender, moss green, and blue.

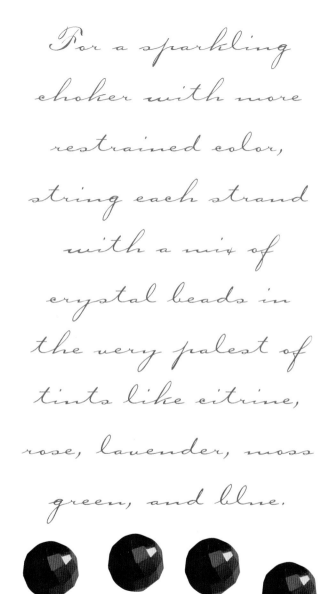

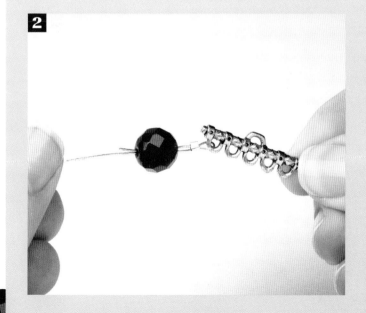

materials

- 6 strands of peridot chips, 6mm wide x 4mm long x 6mm thick (16" strand = 135 chips)
- 12 crimp tubes, gold, size 2
- Rhinestone clasp for three strands, gold
- Transite beading cord

Finished length: 18"

A surprisingly elegant and traditional clasp accents the strands of glass chips.

VARIATION: LETTUCE LEAF

Small peridot chips are the main feature of this six-strand necklace. A decorative gold clasp with dark green rhinestones adds elegance and focus to the substantial choker. "Lettuce Leaf" is made just like "Raspberry Tart" but with a few changes. Restring each purchased strand onto transite. Instead of using end bars and a spring ring clasp, this rhinestone clasp does double duty. Each half of the clasp has three holes, so attach two strands of beads to each hole.

TIP

This elegant rhinestone clasp was harvested from a necklace purchased at a thrift store. The beads were chipped plastic and not worth saving, but the clasp is amazing!

RASPBERRY TART

3. Use a crimp bead and the crimping pliers to attach the other end of the strand to the corresponding outside hole on the second end bar. Tuck the wire end into the last beads.

4. Repeat steps 1–3 to attach the remaining four strands of beads, being sure to attach each end of the strands to the corresponding holes in both end bars.

5. Use a jump ring and both the chain-nose and bent-nose pliers to attach the "figure 8" ring to one end bar. Repeat this step on the other side to attach the spring ring.

TIP
For a straightforward style, wear the necklace with the strands running parallel against the neck. For a more relaxed look, gently twist the necklace before wearing.

jagged edge

Soft pink rose quartz chips resembling the stalactites found in caverns, are strung along this single-strand necklace, featuring a simple symmetrical design. The high-light of "Jagged Edge" is a faceted smoky quartz pendant that is accented with small silver beads. The rose quartz chips gradually become smaller the further away they are from this stunning pendant focal point.

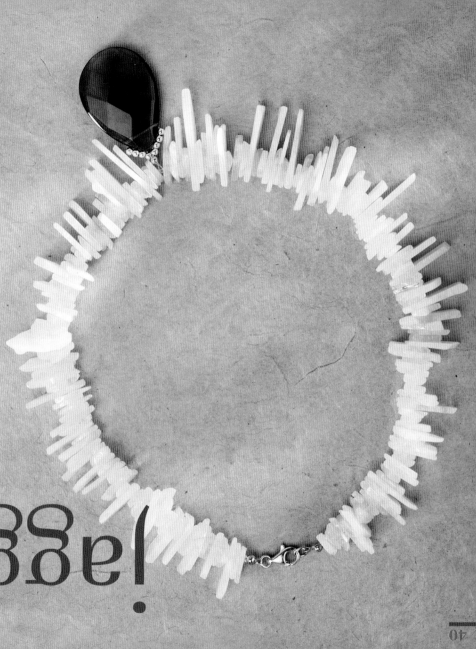

materials

- 1 faceted smoky quartz briolette, 3cm wide x 4cm long x 4mm thick
- 1 strand of rose quartz chips, 8mm wide x 6mm long x 2 thick to 12mm wide x 28mm long x 3mm thick (16" strand = 150 chips)
- 9 round beads, sterling silver, 2mm dia.
- 2 clamshells, sterling silver
- 1 crimp bead, sterling silver, size 1
- 1 jump ring, sterling silver, 16 gauge, 8mm dia.
- 1 lobster clasp, sterling silver, 8mm wide x 12mm long

tools

- Transite
- Wire cutters
- Cyanoacrylate (instant glue) gel
- Bent-nose pliers
- Chain-nose pliers
- Crimping pliers

techniques

- "How to Open and Close a Jump Ring," see pg. 122
- "How to Use a Crimp Tube," see pg. 119
- "How to Use a Clamshell," see pg. 121
- "How to Attach a Clamshell," see pg. 121

Finished length: 17"

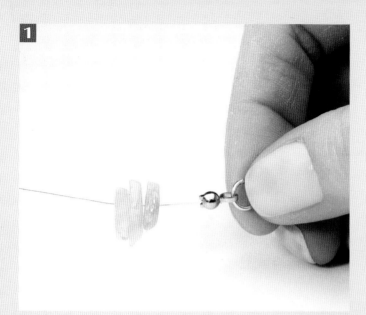

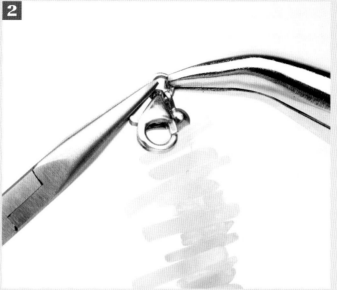

JAGGED EDGE

1. Use the wire cutters to cut a 20-in. length of transite. Attach the transite to a clamshell, and attach the clamshell to the jump ring using the chain-nose and bent-nose pliers. String on a mix of the smallest quartz chips, graduating to larger chips mixed with small until the midpoint. After that, begin to reduce the size of the chips once again.

2. At the other end, attach the transite to the remaining clamshell. Attach the clamshell to the lobster clasp using the bent-nose and chain-nose pliers.

3. Cut a 6-in. length of transite for the pendant. Thread the transite through the quartz pendant, and string four silver beads on each side of the pendant.

4. Bring the ends of the transite together, and thread both ends through the crimp bead.

materials

- 2 slabs "turquoise," pink, 28mm wide x 30mm long x 8mm thick
- 1 slab "turquoise," pink, 42mm wide x 50mm long x 5mm thick
- 12 "turquoise" nuggets, pink, 12mm wide x 18mm long
- 16 round beads, variegated white, 10mm dia.
- 2 clamshells, sterling silver
- 2 crimp tubes, sterling silver, size 1
- 1 hook and eye clasp, sterling silver
- Transite

Finished length: 20"

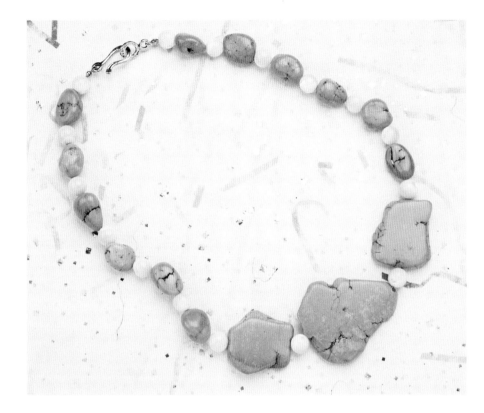

VARIATION: FLAT ROCK

"Flat Rock" is a variation in style from "Jagged Edge," yet doesn't use the same techniques. Rather than thin chips hanging down, large slabs and nuggets of pink "turquoise" sit prominently on this single-strand necklace. The pink "turquoise" alternates with round white beads in this fun confection that's secured with a sterling silver clasp. Simple stringing on a 30-inch length of transite, using crimp beads covered by clamshells, and attaching a silver clasp is all that's required. For directions, see "Wilma" on page 12.

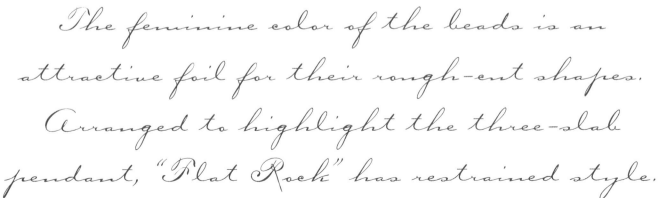

The feminine color of the beads is an attractive foil for their rough-cut shapes. Arranged to highlight the three-slab pendant, "Flat Rock" has restrained style.

JAGGED EDGE

5. Thread on the last silver bead, and slide it down toward the pendant.

6. Wrap both transite ends around the center point of the necklace. Thread the ends back through the last silver bead and the crimp bead. Adjust the transite so the pendant hangs below the chips, allowing the chips to fill the gap made by the attachment, as shown.

7. Use the crimping pliers to secure the crimp bead.

8. Slide the last silver bead over the crimp bead. Use the cutters to trim off the excess transite.

TIP
When using beads or stones that are translucent, use a translucent stringing material like transite.

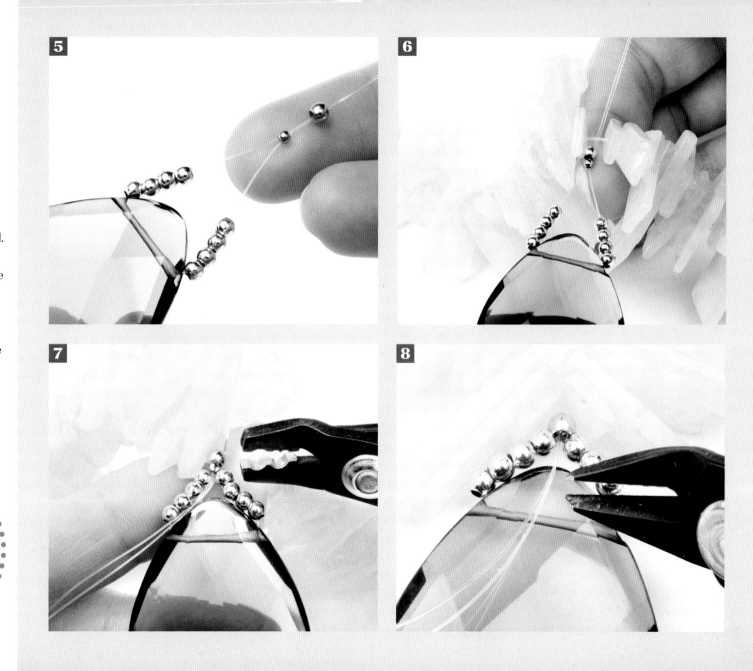

black
orchid

F eaturing three strands of faceted black onyx beads in graduating sizes, "Black Orchid" is accented with gold end bars connected to a hook and chain clasp, which is finished with a small bead. The knotting technique used allows each bead to be individually secured so if the beading thread breaks, beads won't be lost. This exotic necklace is then adorned with three tropical flowers carved from black onyx.

materials

- 3 black onyx tropical flowers, 4cm dia.
- 35 faceted round black onyx beads, 10mm dia.
- 40 faceted round black onyx beads, 8mm dia.
- 59 faceted round black onyx beads, 6mm dia.
- 2 end bars, for three strands, gold, 2cm long
- 3 crimp tubes, gold, size 1
- 6 clamshells, gold
- 1 jump ring, gold, 16 gauge, 4mm dia.
- 1 hook clasp, gold
- 3½" length cable-link chain, gold, 6mm wide x 7mm long
- 2 head pins, gold, 2cm long, 2mm head
- 1 spool of nylon beading thread, in black, size FF

tools

- Ruler ■ Scissors ■ Crystal cement
- Twisted wire beading needle for light-medium beading ■ Tweezers
- Chain-nose pliers ■ Bent-nose pliers ■ Round-nose pliers
- Wire cutters ■ Crimping pliers

techniques

- "How to Attach a Clamshell," see pg. 121

Finished length: 16"

BLACK ORCHID

1. Using two clam shells and 51 of the 6mm beads, make a 14-in. strand following the directions "Creating a Knotted Necklace" (see pg. 123).

2. To make a 15-in. strand, string on a 6mm bead, all of the 8 mm beads, and a 6 mm bead. To make a 16-in. strand, string on a 6mm bead, all of the 10mm beads, and a 6mm bead.

3. Use the chain-nose pliers to attach one end of the 14-in. strand to an outside hole in an end bar.

4. Attach the other end to a corresponding outside hole in the other end bar.

5. Use the chain-nose pliers to attach the 15-in. strand to the center holes and the 16-in. strand to the last outside holes of the end bars.

6. Use two pairs of pliers to attach the clasp's hook to an end bar.

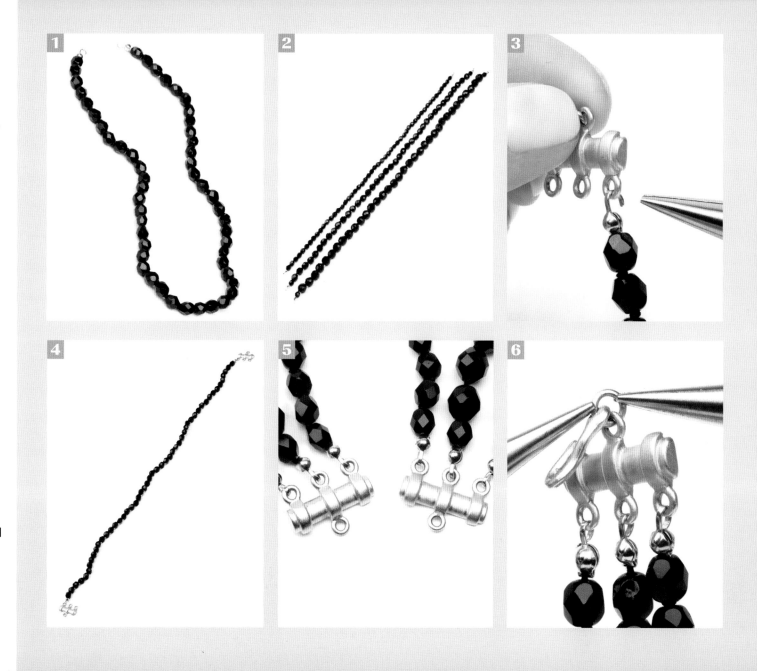

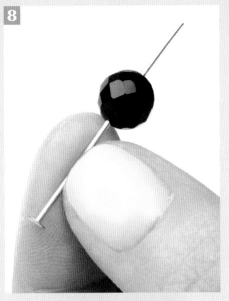

BLACK ORCHID

7. Use the chain-nose and bent-nose pliers to attach the gold chain to the other end bar using a jump ring.

8. To add the bead detail to the chain portion of the clasp, begin by threading one 6mm bead onto the head pin.

9. Use the chain-nose pliers to grasp the head pin ⅛ in. above the bead. Turn the pliers to bend the head pin at a 90° angle.

10. Use the round-nose pliers to grasp the head pin at the bend. Use your fingers to bend the head pin stem around the jaw of the pliers and cross at the front of the stem to form a loop.

11. Use the wire cutters to trim the head pin.

12. Use the chain-nose pliers to open the loop sufficiently to attach it to the last link on the chain. Close the loop.

BLACK ORCHID

13. Attach the flowers as shown on page 44. Cut a 12-in. length of beading thread and have the thread doubled in the beading needle. Insert the needle into the center underside of a flower. Do not pull the thread ends through the flower.

14. String on one 6mm bead.

15. Insert the needle back through the center of the flower.

16. Tie the thread ends together using a double-overhand knot. Cut off the needle.

17. Insert the thread ends into a crimp tube and wrap them around the middle of the 16-in. strand. Thread the ends back through the crimp tube, pull the ends taut to move the flower close to the necklace.

18. Crimp the tube. (See pg. 119.) Repeat steps 13–17 to attach the remaining two flowers.

jet setter

*Our necklace begins with this bead,
and is beaded in the direction of the arrow.

Highly reflective, polished black beads make up this ultra-long single-strand necklace. The beads are a combination of different shapes and textures pairing briolettes, donuts, pipes, and round beads with faceted or smooth surfaces. "Jet Setter" is made as a continuous strand, a technique that requires no clasp. Because it has no clasp with which to contend (and so no beginning or end), the necklace can be worn several different ways.

materials
- 3 faceted onyx briolettes,
  3cm wide x 4cm long x 6mm thick
- 4 onyx donuts,
  13cm dia. x 5mm thick
- 3 onyx pipes,
  10mm dia. x 5.2cm long
- 10 faceted onyx barrels,
  1.5cm wide x 2cm long
- 16 round onyx beads,
  16mm dia.
- 9 faceted round onyx beads,
  14mm dia.
- 26 faceted round onyx beads,
  8mm dia.
- Monofilament, 30 lbs.

tools
- Ruler
- Wire cutters
- Masking tape (optional)
- Cyanoacrylate (instant glue) gel
- Paper clip

techniques
- "How to Make a Single-
  and a Double-Overhand Knot,"
  see pg. 124

Finished length: 42"

JET SETTER

1. Cut a 66-in. length of monofilament. Tie a double knot 12 in. from an end; secure it with glue. Determine the starting point on the necklace photo on page 48. Thread on the first three beads to the left of the starting point.

2. Thread a paper clip onto the 12-in. end of the filament. Thread the short end back through the first bead, trapping the paper clip. Tighten the filament to bring the paper clip close to the bead.

3. On the other side of the bead, tie the filament into a single knot, close to the bead, and add a drop of glue.

4. Thread the same short end through the second bead. Pull the monofilament tight so that the knots are flush against the beads. Repeat step 3.

5. Thread the short end through the third bead, and repeat step 3.

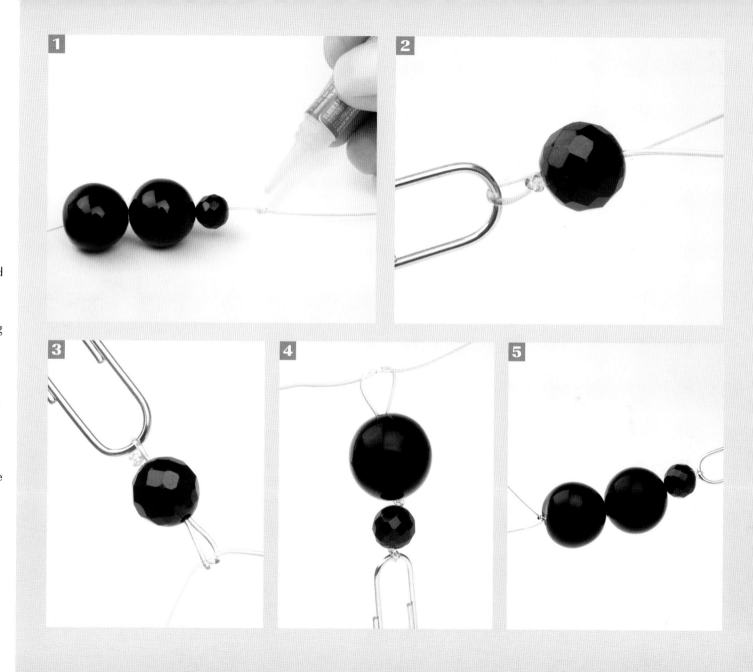

TIP

When making a continuous-strand necklace, be sure that the stringing material will both hold the knots and complement the beads. For example, use monofilament with translucent or transparent beads because the stringing material will show.

VARIATION: PROVENCE

"Provence" has a repeating pattern of dazzling translucent beads in lavender, purple, green, and clear. The necklace is strung with beads in different styles and shapes, and together they create a unique piece of jewelry. Follow the directions for "Jet Setter." String on one bead unless otherwise indicated: round lavender bead, new jade hexagon with four amethyst rondelles in the center, round lavender bead, new jade hexagon with four amethyst rondelles in the center, round lavender bead, rough cut quartz, clear quartz nugget, amethyst rondelle, rectangle of green fluorite, amethyst rondelle, clear quartz nugget, and rough cut quartz. Repeat four times.

materials

- 10 new jade hexagon-shaped donuts, 2.2cm wide x 2.5cm long x 5mm thick
- 10 opaque rough-cut quartz crystal nuggets, 15mm wide x 20mm long x 14mm thick
- 15 faceted round quartz beads, lavender, 14mm dia.
- 5 fluorite rectangles, green, 14mm wide x 20mm long x 6mm thick
- 10 clear quartz nuggets, 10mm wide x 14mm long x 8mm thick
- 50 faceted rondelles, amethyst, 6mm dia. x 3mm long
- Transite

Finished length: 36"

JET SETTER

6. Working toward the left (or counterclockwise), continue to string on the beads of the design without knotting between them, cutting the short end of the filament so that it tucks into the fifth bead. Tuck in the end.

7. When all of the beads are strung, bring the end with the paper clip and the free end of the filament together. (Two more beads are left to go in this photo.)

8. Remove the paper clip from the loop, and thread the end of the filament through the loop.

9. Thread the end of the filament through the first bead on the side opposite the loop.

10. Tie the end into a single-overhand knot, and secure it with a drop of glue. Repeat for the second and third beads. Cut the short end of the filament so that it tucks into the fifth bead. Tuck in the end.

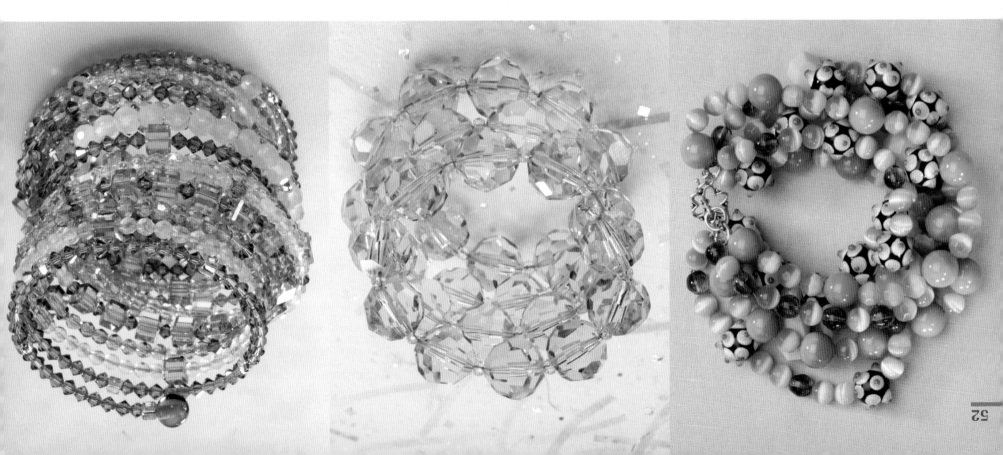

Melondrama
Crushed Ice
Rock Candy
Blue Rain
Margarita
Sugar Cubes
Love Knot
Sunset
Confetti
So Charming
Blue Velvet
Ribbon Candy
Dalmation
Orange Crush
Sea Glass
Ocean
Silver Stream
Souvenir
Paris Café
White Hail

melon drama

A mix of beads in luscious fruit colors is the dramatic hallmark of this bracelet, which comprises six unique strands of glass beads. The quirky standout is done in orange, white, and black lampwork beads, while another strand is a sweet combination of large and small faceted beads in blue and green. Joined together with a flower toggle clasp, this bracelet becomes flirty and fun.

materials
- 4 faceted opaque rondelles, pale blue, 18mm dia. x 11mm long
- 18 opaque round glass beads, watermelon pink, 12mm dia.
- 46 iridescent round glass beads, cantaloupe, 8mm dia.
- 17 clear round glass beads, variegated orange, 8mm dia.
- 49 iridescent round glass beads, lime green, 8mm dia.
- 15 lampwork beads, orange, white, and black, 7mm dia.
- 12 crimp tubes, sterling silver, size 2
- 2 jump rings, sterling silver, 16 gauge, 7mm dia.
- 2 jump rings, sterling silver, 16 gauge, 5mm dia.
- Toggle clasp with flower-shaped ring, 13mm wide
- Beading wire, 0.40mm dia.

tools
- Ruler
- Wire cutters
- Chain-nose pliers
- Bent-nose pliers
- Crimping pliers

techniques
- "How to Open and Close a Jump Ring," see page 122
- "How to Use a Crimp Tube," see page 119

MELONDRAMA

1. Use the wire cutters to cut six 12-in. lengths of beading wire. Use a crimp tube and crimping pliers to attach a 7mm jump ring to the end of one length.

2. Following the beading layout, choose one strand and string on the corresponding beads. Thread a crimp tube onto the end of the strand, and attach another 7mm jump ring using the crimping pliers.

beading layout

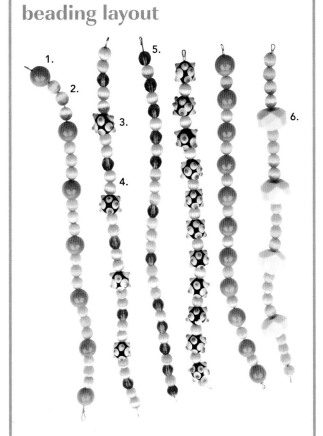

1. Opaque round glass bead, watermelon pink, 8mm dia.
2. Iridescent round glass bead, lime green, 8mm dia.
3. Lampwork bead, orange, white, and black, 7mm
4. Iridescent round glass bead, orange, 8mm
5. Clear round glass bead, variegated orange, 8mm dia.
6. Faceted opaque rondelle, pale blue, 18 mm dia. x 11mm long

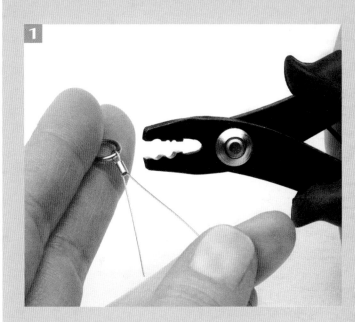

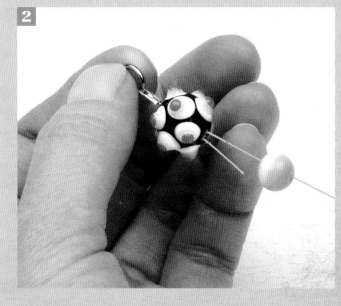

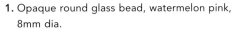

materials

- 12 raw quartz chunks, ½" cubes
- 9 clear quartz chips, ¾" wide
- 10 clear glass discs, with blue centers, 10mm dia. x 3mm thick
- 28 clear quartz claw briolettes, 8mm wide x 3mm long x 6mm thick
- 20 opaque cracked quartz claw briolettes, white, 8mm wide x 3mm long x 6mm thick
- 34 quartz rondelles, pale blue, 3mm dia. x 4mm long
- 7 clear cracked quartz oval beads, 2.3cm wide x 3.5cm long
- 29 clear crystal seed beads, size 11
- 10 crimp tubes, sterling silver, size 2
- 2 jump rings, sterling silver, 16 gauge, 7mm dia.
- 2 jump rings, sterling silver, 16 gauge, 5mm dia.
- Toggle clasp, sterling silver, 15mm dia.
- Beading wire, 0.40mm dia.

VARIATION: CRUSHED ICE

A mix of clear, crazed, and frosted beads gives the impression that this five-strand bracelet is made from chunks of ice. There are natural crystals that appear to have broken off from a larger crystal formation, raw quartz cubes with rough surfaces, and irregularly-shaped chips in milky white. Highly polished, oversized quartz beads reveal hairline cracks that lend sparkling textural contrast. Light blue rondelles cast a haze of color onto the white beads.

beading sequence

Strand 1:
Alternate between one raw quartz chunk and one pale blue rondelle.

Strand 2:
Alternate between one quartz chip and one glass disc.

Strand 3:
Alternate between one clear quartz claw briolette and one seed bead.

Strand 4:
String on all opaque cracked quartz claw briolettes.

Strand 5:
String on all cracked quartz oval beads

MELONDRAMA

3. Using a crimp tube and the crimping pliers, attach another length of beading wire to the jump ring as in step 1. Follow the directions in step 2 to complete the strand. Continue as before to complete the remaining four strands.

4. Open a 5mm jump ring, and thread it through the 7mm jump ring and the toggle clasp ring. Close the jump ring using the chain-nose and bent-nose pliers.

5. Repeat step 4 to attach the toggle clasp bar to the other end.

TIP
Each finished strand of beads is approximately 9 inches long. Because the beads have varying diameters and each strand has different beads, each strand will be a slightly different finished length.

rock candy

materials
- 36 faceted clear round beads, pink, 16mm dia.
- 37 faceted clear rondelles, pink, 4mm dia. x 3mm long
- Coil of memory wire, bright silver, heavy bracelet weight

tools
- Wire cutters
- Chain-nose pliers
- Emery cloth

O versized faceted crystals in water-clear pink are threaded onto loops and loops of memory wire to create a continuous chunky spiral of beads that sparkles with style. Easy and fun to make, all you need to do is thread the beads on a wire that always "remembers" its original shape, making sure to crimp the wire at both ends to secure the beads.

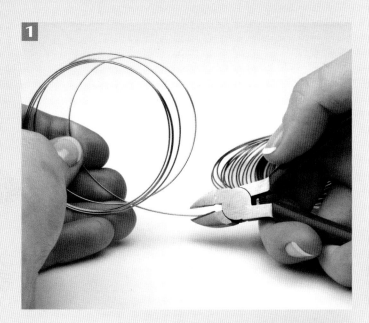

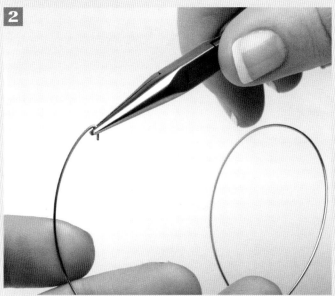

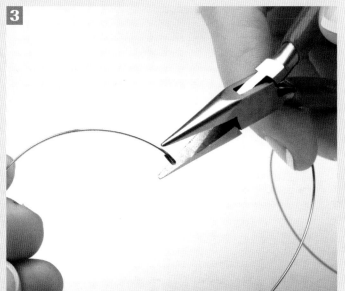

ROCK CANDY

1. Count four complete loops of memory wire, and use the wire cutters to cut the loops from the coil. Use emery cloth to smooth the cut ends.

2. Use the tips of the chain-nose pliers to bend the wire ⅛ in. from one end.

3. Use a wider section of the pliers' jaws to squeeze the end flat to the wire.

4. Thread the opposite end of the wire through one rondelle and one round bead. Slide the beads along the wire until they reach the bent end.

Consider wearing the "Rock Candy" cuff together with "Blue Rain." The bracelets look great when worn with a party dress or a lacy camisole.

materials

- 10 faceted clear briolettes, blue, 15mm dia. x 26mm long
- 8 faceted clear ovals, pink, 6mm wide x 8mm long
- 350 faceted clear ovals, blue, 3mm dia. x 4mm long
- 12 opaque round beads, blue, 3mm dia.
- Coil of memory wire, bright silver, heavy bracelet weight

VARIATION: BLUE RAIN

Here, seven loops of memory wire are threaded with crystal beads in watery colors to create this elegant cuff. The beading pattern echoes the delicate hues of a gentle spring shower with large crystal teardrops suggesting a stream of rain drops.

Crimp one end of the wire following the directions for "Rock Candy." Lay out all the beads in a straight line, arranging them in a pleasing order. Thread them on the memory wire. When all the beads have been threaded, crimp the end of the wire.

ROCK CANDY

5. Continue this beading pattern using the remaining beads. When all the beads are on the wire, there will be approximately 1 in. of wire unbeaded.

6. Use the tip of the pliers to measure approximately ⅛ in. from the last bead. Then use the wire cutters to measure another ⅛ in. Cut off the excess wire.

7. Use the chain-nose pliers to bend the end of the wire and squeeze the end flat as in steps 2–3.

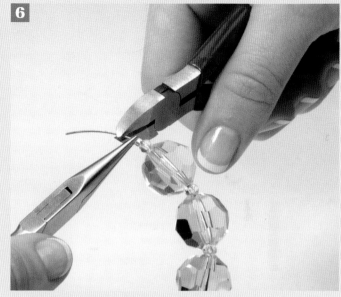

TIP

The greater the number of loops of memory wire, the greater the number of beads needed to achieve the chunky look. Remember also, the heavier the bead, the heavier the bracelet.

margarita

Reminiscent of a cool summer drink, rough chunks of quartz crystal and pale green faceted beads in new jade bring to mind a frothy lime concoction in a chilled glass rimmed with rock salt. This creation features three strands of chunky beads, strung in a repeating pattern, which are combined with rhinestone-accented silver bar clasps. The soft shifts in color play up the variety of shape and texture. A sterling silver lobster clasp completes the piece.

materials

- 13 round faceted beads, pale green new jade, 20mm dia.
- 14 rough quartz crystal nuggets, clear, 10mm wide x 13mm long x 12mm thick
- 30 round faceted dyed quartz crystal beads, green, 6mm dia.
- 2 rhinestone accented end bars, for three strands, silver
- 6 crimp beads, sterling silver, size 1
- 6 clamshells, silver
- 1 jump ring, sterling silver, 16 gauge, 7mm dia.
- 1 jump ring, sterling silver, 16 gauge, 5mm dia.
- 1 lobster clasp, sterling silver, 7mm x 14mm
- Monofilament, 20 lbs

tools

- Ruler
- Wire cutters
- Crimping pliers
- Chain-nose pliers
- Bent-nose pliers

techniques

- "How to Open and Close a Jump Ring," see page 122
- "How to Use a Clamshell to Cover a Crimp Bead," see page 122
- "How to Use a Crimp Tube," see page 119

MARGARITA

1. Use wire cutters to cut three 10-in. strands of monofilament. Set two aside. Use a crimp bead and a clamshell to attach one end of the strand to an outside hole of one end bar.

2. Following the beading layout, string beads onto the strand. Thread a clamshell and a crimp bead onto the end of the strand, and attach it to the corresponding outside hole of the second end bar.

beading layout

1. Rough quartz crystal nugget, clear, 10mm wide x 13mm long x 12mm thick
2. Round faceted bead, pale green new jade, 20mm dia.
3. Round faceted dyed quartz, green, 6mm dia.

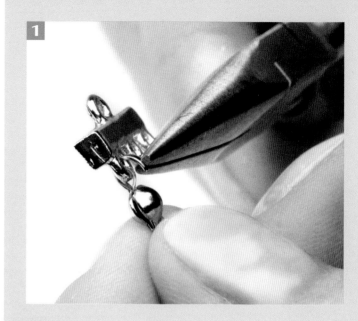

1

2

TIP
Note the center strand of the beading layout. Its bead pattern begins with the new jade bead instead of the quartz. This prevents the jade beads of the three strands from rubbing against one another.

Rough quartz chunks are made glamorous by the fancy faceted crystal beads and filigree gold clasp.

materials

- 19 rough quartz crystal nuggets, pink, 15mm wide x 20mm long x 14mm thick
- 28 faceted crystal rondelles, clear, 5mm dia. x 4mm long
- 6 round beads, gold, 8mm dia.
- 32 round beads, gold, 2mm dia.
- 2 decorative bar ends, for three strands, gold
- 6 crimp beads, gold, size 1
- 6 clamshells, gold
- 1 jump ring, gold, 16 gauge, 7mm dia.
- 1 jump ring, gold, 16 gauge, 5mm dia.
- 1 spring ring clasp, gold, 12mm dia.
- Beading wire, 0.32mm dia.

VARIATION: SUGAR CUBES

Rough-cut quartz nuggets (resembling pink sugar in the raw) are juxtaposed with delicate gold beads, shimmering faceted crystal rondelles, and a decorative gold-tone scrollwork clasp. The beads combine to make a surprisingly elegant bracelet. Created in the same manner as "Margarita," this bracelet also has three strands of beads attached to bar ends. To make a bracelet with more strands, use bar ends with five- or six-strand attachments.

The appeal of this bracelet lies in the contrast among the design elements. Rough and smooth beads, small and large, are placed together, distinguished by the shift from light jade to dark jade green.

MARGARITA

3. Repeat steps 1–2 to attach the two remaining strands to the end bar; string on the remaining beads; and secure the strands to the second end bar.

4. Use the chain-nose and bent-nose pliers to open the 5mm jump ring. Thread the jump ring through the top hole of one end bar and the lobster clasp; close the jump ring. Use the same technique to secure the 7mm jump ring to the top hole of the second end bar.

love knot

materials

- 640 opaque round dyed coral beads, light blue, 4mm dia.
- 16 crimp tubes, sterling silver, size 2
- 5 jump rings, sterling silver, 16 gauge, 8mm dia.
- Lobster clasp, sterling silver, 8mm wide x 16mm long
- Beading wire, 0.32mm dia.

tools

- Ruler
- Wire cutters
- Crimping pliers
- Chain-nose pliers
- Bent-nose pliers

techniques

- "How to Open and Close a Jump Ring," see page 122.
- "How to Use a Crimp Tube," see page 119.

E ight strands of pale blue dyed coral beads gathered onto jump rings make up "Love Knot," a bracelet that is surprisingly easy to create. The bracelet is made extra long to allow a knot to be tied in the center, adding visual interest to its monochromatic look. By clustering multiple strands, small beads create a big impact. For a different look, use one strand of large, round beads.

LOVE KNOT

1. Use the wire cutters to cut eight 14-in. lengths of beading wire. Use a crimp tube and crimping pliers to attach two jump rings to the end of one wire.

2. String 80 beads onto the wire. Thread a crimp tube onto the end of the wire, and attach two more jump rings using the crimping pliers.

3. Repeat steps 1–2 for the remaining seven strands, using the same jump rings.

4. Open the remaining jump ring, and thread it through both jump rings at one end of the bracelet and the lobster clasp. Close the jump ring using the chain-nose and bent-nose pliers.

materials

- 172 rectangular carnelian beads, 5mm wide x 7mm long x 3mm thick
- 240 dyed freshwater pearls, gold, 3mm wide x 5mm long x 2mm thick
- 32 diamond-shaped faceted crystal rondelles, burnt orange, 4mm dia. x 4mm long
- 16 crimp tubes, gold, size 2
- 5 jump rings, gold, 16 gauge, 8mm dia.
- Lobster clasp, gold, 8mm wide x 16mm long
- Beading wire, 0.32mm dia.

VARIATION: SUNSET

Combine four strands of carnelian beads with four strands of freshwater pearls and gather together with gold jump rings and finish with a gold lobster clasp. The deep orange of the carnelian beads brings to mind a summer sunset and pleasantly complements the lighter-colored freshwater pearls. Make "Sunset" the same way as "Love Knot" with the addition of two crystal rondelles at the beginning and end of each strand.

The freshwater pearls and carnelian beads are reminiscent of treasures found on the shore at day's end.

LOVE KNOT

5. To create the knot, begin by placing the bracelet open on a flat surface.

6. Cross one end over the other.

7. Insert one end into the space at the center.

8. Pull the ends gently to create the knot.

TIP
Try combining beads of different shapes and colors for a whole new look!

confetti

T his bracelet gives its wearer a fun way to change charms at will. The charms used are made from thin, iridescent shells cut into discs and painted with polka-dots along with ones cut into flower shapes and dyed bright colors. The contrasting shapes lend playful style. A lobster clasp secured to each charm allows them to be easily added or removed from the chain-link bracelet. A floral ribbon woven through the chain adds the finishing touch.

materials

- 8 shell discs with polka-dots, 3cm dia.
  - 2 pink
  - 2 yellow
  - 2 green
  - 2 orange
- 16 flower-shaped shells, 2cm dia.
  - 4 yellow
  - 4 orange
  - 4 green
  - 4 pink
- 1' flat link chain, sterling silver, 12-gauge round wire, 8mm wide x 14mm long
- 26 jump rings, silver, 16 gauge, 6mm dia.
- 24 lobster clasps, silver, 8mm wide x 15mm long
- Toggle clasp with flower-shaped ring, silver, 13mm wide
- ½ yd. satin polka-dot ribbon, orange with white polka-dots, ⅛" wide

tools

- Ruler
- Chain cutters
- Chain-nose pliers
- Bent-nose pliers
- Scissors

techniques

- "How to Open and Close a Jump Ring," see page 122

CONFETTI

1. Use the memory-wire cutters to cut a 7-in. length of chain.

2. Open a jump ring, and thread it through the last link of the chain and the toggle clasp ring. Close the jump ring using both pliers. Use a jump ring to attach the toggle clasp bar to the other end of the chain.

3. Thread an open jump ring through a polka-dot disc and a lobster clasp; close the jump ring. Repeat this step for the remaining polka-dot discs and flowers.

TIP
The best way to add charms is to place the chain flat on a work surface, making sure there are no twists in the chain. Add the charms only along the bottom edge of the links of chain. This will ensure that all of the charms hang properly when the bracelet is worn.

materials

- 6 round painted glass beads, black with pink roses, 20mm dia.
- 7 rectangular cubes with engraved roses, gold, 9mm wide x 10mm long x 9mm thick
- 13 assorted charms:
  - Locket, gold ▪ Pea pod
  - Cross, gold ▪ 2 monogrammed letters, rhinestone and silver
  - Leaf, gold ▪ Dancing girl, gold
  - 2 monogrammed hearts, black enamel with gold ▪ "I LOVE NY," gold ▪ Statue of Liberty medallion, gold ▪ Oval floral pendant, gold
  - Love knot, gold
- 1' large cable link chain, gold, 8-gauge half-round wire, 7mm wide x 7mm long
- 12 bead caps, gold, 8mm dia.
- 2 jump rings, gold, 14 gauge, 8mm
- 1 spring ring, gold, 15mm dia.
- 13 lobster clasps, gold, 6mm wide x 10mm long
- 13 jump rings, gold, 16 gauge, 4mm
- 13 jump rings, gold, 16 gauge, 6mm
- Wire, gold, 22 gauge

additional tools

- Wire cutters
- Round-nose pliers

additional techniques

- "How to Make a Wrapped Wire Loop," see page 120

The juxta-position of plump beads painted black with delicate roses and the sentimental gold charms creates tex-tural contrast and appeal-ing style.

VARIATION: SO CHARMING

This flashy designer copy and intentionally "over-the-top" charm bracelet boasts a heavy gold chain, painted black enamel beads with bead caps, and gold cubes with engraved roses on all four sides. It is important to note that you must first fit the black beads and gold cubes with wrapped wire loops made from headpins; then attach them to the links in the bracelet using jump rings. Attach the remaining gold charms directly to the bracelet using jump rings and lobster clasps.

CONFETTI

4. Following the beading layout, use the lobster clasps to attach the polka-dot discs and flowers to the chain.

5. With the bracelet open on a flat surface, weave the ribbon through the chain link. Have enough ribbon at both ends so that when the bracelet is worn, there is sufficient length to tie a bow.

beading layout

1. Shell disk with polka-dots in pink
2. Flower-shaped shell in yellow
3. Flower-shaped shell in orange
4. Shell disk with polka-dots in yellow
5. Flower-shaped disk in green
6. Flower-shaped disk in red
7. Shell disk with polka-dots in green
8. Shell disk with polka-dots in orange

blue velvet

materials
- Rhinestone belt buckle, pink, blue, green, yellow, and purple, 3" dia.
- ⅓ yd. velvet ribbon, blue, 2" wide
- Sewing thread to match ribbon
- White craft glue

tools
- Ruler
- Scissors
- Straight pins
- Sewing machine

Inspired by a bracelet created by a top couture designer, "Blue Velvet" features an impressive rhinestone belt buckle and a wide blue velvet ribbon. The belt buckle is in the shape of a star and fashioned from round and colorful marquise rhinestones. Blue velvet ribbon threaded through the belt buckle provides the foundation for this eye-catching, adjustable bracelet.

1. Cut an 11-in. length of ribbon.

2. With the belt buckle and ribbon wrong side facing up, thread the ribbon under the first crossbar on the buckle.

3. Have 3 in. of ribbon extending beyond the crossbar. Turn the ribbon end under ¼ in.

4. Fold the ribbon end onto the ribbon, and secure it with a straight pin, making sure to retain the fold in the end.

TIP

Use your imagination when choosing your belt buckle. They come in a wide variety of styles.

Sewing is a better option than gluing because the glue tends to seep through the ribbon and leave a mark on the right side.

VARIATION: RIBBON CANDY

This cheerful bracelet highlighted by a prominent plastic buckle in transparent aqua blue is the perfect addition to any summer outfit. A wide, colorful grosgrain ribbon with orange, red, and aqua stripes perfectly complements the buckle and allows for easy adjustment to any wrist size. Consider purchasing a number of ribbons and changing the wristband as often as you like. It's an inexpensive way of quickly getting a whole new look.

materials
- Clear plastic round belt buckle, aqua blue, 2" dia.
- ⅓ yd. striped grosgrain ribbon, orange, red, and, aqua, 2" wide
- Sewing thread to match ribbon
- White craft glue

TIP
Grosgrain ribbon is just one option. Try velvet, satin, or organdy ribbons, or even lace trims. They are available in so many colors and patterns that you'll be sure to find the perfect complement to any belt buckle.

5. With matching thread in the machine, sew across the ribbon a scant ⅛ in. from the end fold.

6. Thread the other end of the ribbon through the second crossbar of the buckle, and adjust it to fit. Trim the ribbon end into a swallow's tail, as shown. Run a thin line of white glue along the raw edges of the ribbon to prevent them from fraying.

TIP
Belt buckles are a great solution when making a big chunky bracelet but don't forget to check out craft and trim stores for any item that may function in the same way!

Velvet ribbon can easily slip when being sewn, so be sure to use straight pins.

dalmatian

So simple and stunning, the black and white "Dalmatian" is a classic addition to anyone's wardrobe. This easy-to-make bracelet features large, faceted black onyx and white agate beads. It has a single strand of large beads attached to jump rings at either end. A black and white polka-dot organdy ribbon is threaded through the jump rings and tied into a bow for an unexpected closure that is adjustable to any wrist size.

materials

- 4 round faceted beads, black onyx, 24mm dia.
- 4 round faceted beads, white agate, 24mm dia.
- 2 jump rings, sterling silver, 16 gauge, 8mm dia.
- 2 crimp tubes, sterling silver, size 2
- ½ yard organdy polka dot ribbon, black and white, 1 in. wide
- Monofilament, 30 lbs

tools

- Ruler
- Wire cutter
- Crimping pliers
- Scissors

techniques

- "How to Use a Crimp Tube," see page 119

DALMATIAN

1. Cut a 12-in. length of monofilament using wire cutters. Attach a jump ring to one end, using a crimp tube and the crimping pliers.

2. String on the beads, alternating between black and white.

3. Use a crimp tube and crimping pliers to attach a jump ring to the other end.

TIP
Although organdy ribbon adds a touch of sheer elegance, don't over-look grosgrain or velvet ribbons. Black and white beads look great with anything, so try a ribbon in a striking color, like vibrant red.

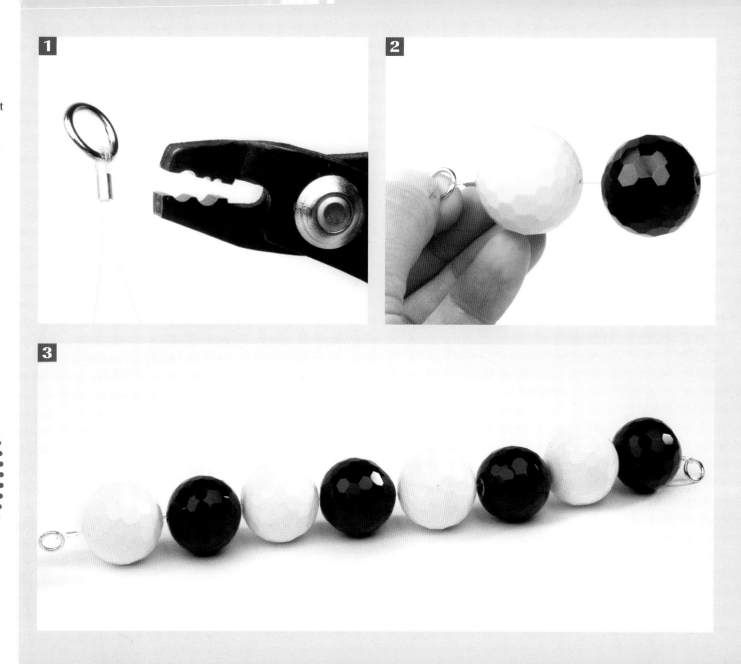

79

materials

- 6 round painted glass beads, black
- 24 round plastic beads, orange, 18mm dia.
- 4 crimp tubes, sterling silver, size 2
- 4 jump rings, sterling silver, 16 gauge, 8mm dia.
- ½ yard striped grosgrain ribbon, white and orange, ⅞" wide
- Monofilament, 30lbs

VARIATION: ORANGE CRUSH

Two strands of large orange beads (resembling colorful orange gumballs!), are joined together with a bright orange and white striped ribbon. The bracelet is made exactly like "Dalmatian," but instead of making one strand, make two. Thread the grosgrain ribbon through all of the jump rings and tie it into a bow. Make as many strands as you like but keep in mind, as the number of strands increase, the size of the beads may need to decrease.

TIP
For a nautical look, use navy or white beads along with a navy and white striped ribbon.

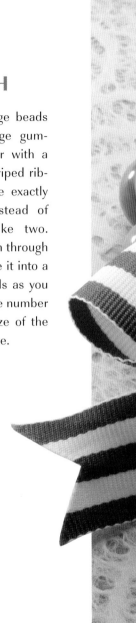

DALMATIAN

4. Bring the ends of the bracelet together and thread the ribbon through both jump rings.

5. Tie the ribbon ends into a bow, adjusting the ribbon to fit your wrist. Trim off excess ribbon.

With the wide variety of beads available, you'll have no trouble finding ones that suit your personal style.

sea glass

This sophisticated cuff is fashioned from 16 coils of memory wire strung with chips of aquamarine that resemble the sea-worn glass found along sandy beaches. A simple bend in the wire at both ends keeps the beads securely in place. Memory wire holds its shape, so the bracelet can be wrapped up the wrist or overlapped on itself for more girth. Adjust the number of coils, as desired, to create a larger or smaller bracelet.

materials
- 7 strands of aquamarine chips, pale blue, 6mm wide x 4mm long x 6mm thick (16" strand = 135 chips)
- Memory wire, bright silver, heavy bracelet weight, 16 coils min.

tools
- Memory wire cutters
- Chain-nose pliers
- Crimping pliers
- Emery cloth

1

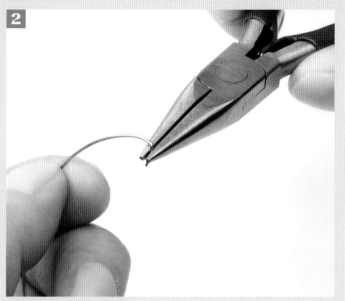

2

SEA GLASS

1. Count 16 complete loops of memory wire, and use the memory-wire cutters to cut the loops from the coil. Smooth the cut ends using an emery cloth.

2. Use the tips of the chain-nose pliers to bend the wire ⅛ in. from one end.

3. Use a wider section of the pliers' jaws to squeeze the end flat to the wire.

3

Chips of sea glass catch the light at different angles, causing the bracelet to glow and sparkle.

Cobalt blue and gold also combine beautifully. Mix opaque and transparent beads for added texture.

materials

- 11 round glass beads, turquoise, 8mm dia.
- 1 round glass bead, green, 8mm dia.
- 50 faceted round glass beads, translucent white, 6mm dia.
- 1 package Austrian crystal cubes, leaf green, 6mm (36 per package)
- 1 package Austrian crystal cubes, turquoise, 4mm (72 per package)
- 2 packages Austrian crystal bicones, teal, 3mm (144 per package)
- 1 package Austrian crystal bicones, turquoise, 3mm (144 per package)
- 1 package Austrian crystal bicones, moss green, 3mm (144 per package)
- 4 packages Austrian crystal rondelles, light blue, 3mm dia. x 4mm long (72 per package)
- 3 packages Austrian crystal rondelles, leaf green, 3mm dia. x 4mm long (72 per package)
- 1 package Austrian crystal rondelles, translucent white, 3mm dia. x 4mm long (72 per package)
- Memory wire, bright silver, heavy bracelet weight, 19 coils min.
- Beading cement

VARIATION: OCEAN

Nineteen coils of shimmering Austrian crystals in ocean colors come together to create a magnificent cuff bracelet. Strung in a random fashion, each coil hosts its own color before blending into another shade or type of bead. Most of the coils are strung with bicones and rondelles. Larger cubes and round beads appear sporadically. The design idea was to create a cuff that looks like 19 separate bangles that are collected together. This bracelet is different from "Sea Glass" in that there are large beads at both ends. After bending the wire ends, apply a drop of beading glue to each and insert them into 8mm round beads, one for each end. Let the glue dry.

SEA GLASS

4. Thread the opposite end of the wire through one chip. Slide the chip along the wire until it reaches the bent end. Continue to add chips until the wire is covered. Leave approximately 1 in. of wire unbeaded at the end.

5. Use the tip of the pliers to measure approximately ⅛ in. from the last chip. Then use the memory-wire cutters to measure another ⅛ in. Cut off the excess wire.

6. Use the chain-nose pliers to bend the end of the wire, and squeeze the end flat as in steps 2–3.

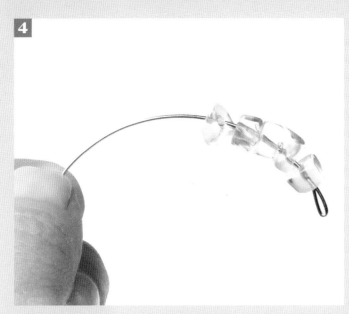

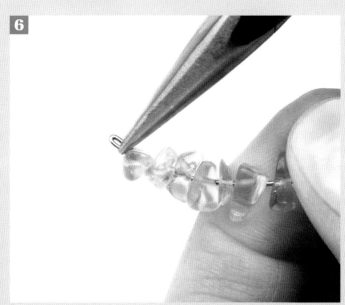

TIP
To avoid tangling when using many loops of memory wire, slide about 10 chips on the end and rotate all the coils of wire either toward or away from you and at a slight angle until all the chips slide right down the wire.

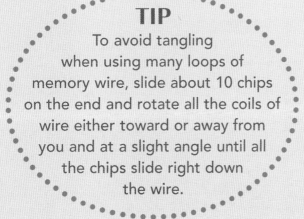

silver stream

This all-silver chain creation features 12 delicate, fine-link chains gathered together with bar clasps. The centerpiece of this bracelet is a charm of icy cracked quartz crystal, which is suspended on a head pin and accented with silver discs above and below it. The charm is attached to the bracelet with a wrapped wire loop. All the design elements create an elegant and sophisticated bracelet.

materials
- 1 clear cracked quartz oval, 2.3cm wide x 3.5cm long
- 7' cable-link chain, sterling silver, 20-gauge round wire, 2mm wide x 3mm long
- 2 end bars, for three strands, sterling silver, 12mm long
- 2 discs, sterling silver, 6mm dia. x 3mm thick
- 1 head pin, sterling silver, 18-gauge wire, 7cm long with a 3mm-wide head
- 1 jump ring, sterling silver, 16 gauge, 8mm dia.
- 2 jump rings, sterling silver, 16 gauge, 7mm dia.
- 7 jump rings, sterling silver, 16 gauge, 6mm dia.
- 1 lobster clasp, sterling silver, 8mm wide x 16mm long

tools
- Ruler
- Wire cutters
- Chain-nose pliers
- Bent-nose pliers
- Round-nose pliers
- Emery cloth

techniques
- "How to Open and Close a Jump Ring," see pg. 122
- "How to Make a Wrapped Wire Loop," see pg. 120

SILVER STREAM

1. Use the wire cutters to cut 12 7-in. lengths of chain. Group the chains into three sets of four chains.

2. Thread one set of four chains onto a 6mm jump ring.

3. Use the chain-nose and bent-nose pliers to attach the jump ring to an outside hole in an end bar. Use another 6mm jump ring to attach the other ends of the four chains to a corresponding outside hole in the other end bar.

TIP
When cutting chain, work on a flat surface and use a ruler. This will ensure that every piece of chain will be the same length.

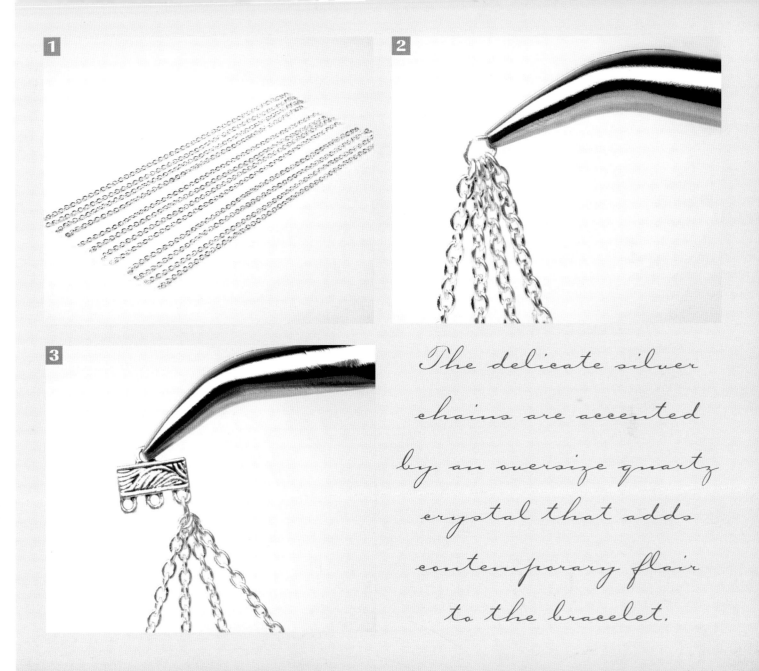

The delicate silver chains are accented by an oversize quartz crystal that adds contemporary flair to the bracelet.

VARIATION: SOUVENIR

This bracelet, which could be mistaken for a precious family heirloom, is fashioned from three strands of fancy-link gold chain gathered together on bar clasps. The charms are polished stones in different colors and shapes. Each stone is placed on a gold head pin with small gold accent beads on top and bottom. The head pin is then formed into a wrapped wire loop, and the five stones are attached to the bracelet with a jump ring.

TIP
For another look, string several smaller beads on each head pin. Or try attaching the charms all the way around the bracelet using the wire loops and jump rings.

materials

- 5 polished stones approximately 2mm x 2mm:
  - 1 pale green square
  - 1 clear round
  - 1 lavender nugget
  - 1 aqua nugget
  - 1 green nugget
- 2' flat chain link, gold, 6mm wide x 8mm long
- 2 end bars, for three strands, gold, 18mm long
- 10 round beads, gold, 4mm dia.
- 5 head pins, gold, 20-gauge wire, 2" long with 1mm-dia. head
- 4 jump rings, gold, 16 gauge, 8mm dia.
- 6 jump rings, gold, 16 gauge, 6mm dia.
- 2 jump rings, gold, 16 gauge, 5mm dia.
- 1 lobster clasp, gold, 8mm wide x 14mm long

For a different look, substitute gold chains and findings. Accent the bracelet with a large gold charm or several gold nuggets.

4. Repeat steps 2–3 to attach the remaining sets of chain.

5. Thread a 7mm jump ring through the top hole of one end bar and the lobster clasp. Use both pliers to close the jump ring.

6. Follow the directions on page 120 to create a quartz charm with a wrapped loop. Secure a 6mm jump ring to the top hole of the second end bar. Attach a 7mm jump ring to the 6mm jump ring. Then thread the 8mm jump ring through the loop of the quartz charm and the 7mm jump ring. Close the jump ring.

paris café

Highly polished baby pink round beads and faceted soft blue rondelles create a pastel backdrop for deep raspberry nuggets and whimsical lampwork beads. Each adds surprising pattern and texture to the bracelet. Reminiscent of the colors associated with Marie Antoinette, the beads are suspended on loops made of head pins and grouped in a random design of color and shape.

materials

- 10 opaque bean-shaped nuggets, deep raspberry, 14mm wide x 20mm long x 10mm thick
- 12 faceted opaque rondelles, pale blue, 18mm dia. x 11mm long
- 22 opaque round beads, pink, 16mm dia.
- 8 lampwork beads, turquoise blue, yellow, brown, and white, 14mm dia.
- 40 faceted opaque ovals, turquoise blue, 4mm wide x 5mm long x 3mm thick
- 74 discs, sterling silver, 1mm–1.5mm dia.
- 2 jump rings, sterling silver, 12 gauge, 8mm dia.
- Spring ring clasp, sterling silver, 16mm dia.
- 7" cable-link chain, sterling silver, 5mm dia. links
- 52 head pins, sterling silver, 4cm long

tools

- Chain-nose pliers
- Bent-nose pliers
- Round-nose pliers
- Wire cutters

techniques

- "How to Make a Wrapped Wire Loop," see page 120.

PARIS CAFÉ

1. Open two jump rings. Use chain-
and bent-nose pliers and one jump
ring to attach the clasp to an end
link of the chain. Close the jump
ring. Attach the second open jump
ring to the end link at the other end
of the chain. Close the jump ring,
and set the bracelet aside.

2. Insert a head pin through one blue
nugget and two turquoise blue oval
beads. To begin the wrapped loop,
use the chain-nose pliers to grasp
the head pin ⅛ in. above the top
bead. Hold the beads with the
other hand, and turn the pliers
away from you to bend the head
pin stem at a 90° angle.

3. Use the round-nose pliers to grasp
the head pin at the bend. Use your
fingers to bend the head-pin stem
around the jaw of the pliers and
then cross at the front of the stem
to make a loop.

4. Insert the end of the head pin into
the second link on the chain after
the jump ring as shown.

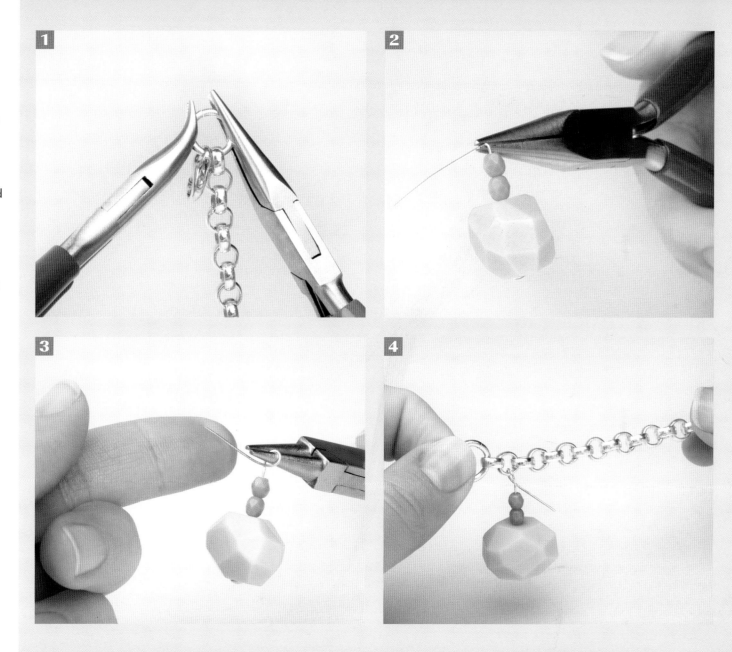

VARIATION: WHITE HAIL

Perfect for any season, this monochromatic blizzard of polished round beads makes a great statement when worn with either winter whites or summer brights. This bracelet is created using the same technique as "Paris Café."

Begin by connecting two beads to every other link in the chain. Then continue to add more beads wherever you wish to see beads clustered more densely. The beads on the bracelet shown are concentrated most densely in the middle.

Practice making wrapped wire loops on inexpensive soft wire to master the technique before using the head pins to make the loops on the beads for this bracelet.

materials

- 100 round beads, variegated white, 10mm dia.
- 2 jump rings, sterling silver, 12 gauge, 8mm dia.
- Spring ring clasp, sterling silver, 16mm dia.
- 7" cable-link chain, sterling silver, 5mm-dia. links
- 100 head pins, sterling silver, 3cm long

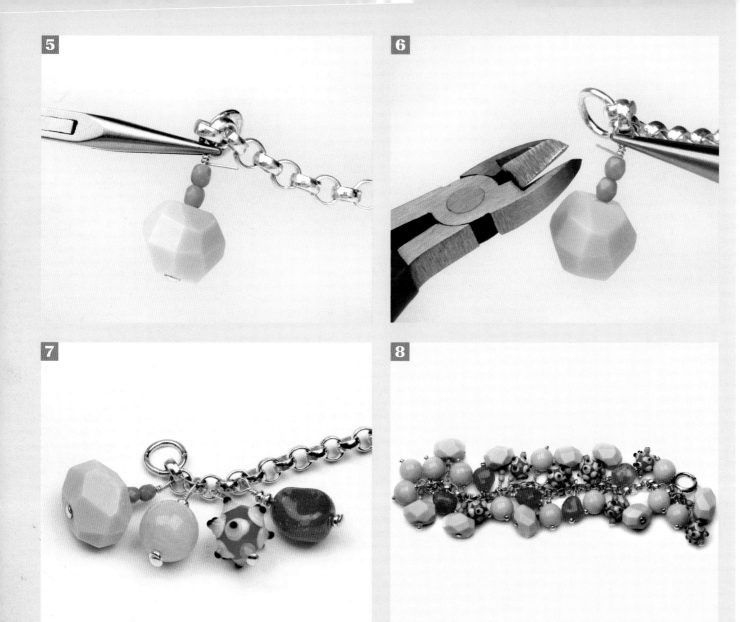

PARIS CAFÉ

5. Grasp the loop with the flat-nose pliers, and use your fingers or the bent-nose pliers, if necessary, to wrap the head-pin end three times around the stem, moving from the loop down toward the first bead.

6. Use the wire cutters to snip off the excess wire. Use pliers to squeeze the cut end flush against the stem.

7. Repeat steps 2–6 to attach the following to the chain: a pink bead with a silver disc below and above it, a lampwork bead with a turquoise blue oval bead below and above it, and a raspberry nugget with one silver disc below and two silver discs above the bead.

8. Continue to attach the beads to the links in the chain, distributing them in a random pattern or as desired.

9. Optional: For a chunkier look, double the number of beads, attaching two beads to every other link.

Note: the additional beads will lessen the movement of the surrounding beads.

Cosmopolitan
Manhattan
Wrap Star
Ice Cube
Cherry Bomb
Fireworks
On the Rocks
Trio
In Bloom
Rock 'N' Blues

cosmopolitan

A large emerald-cut pink "tourmaline" is the center-piece of "Cosmo," a sparkling ring made from a pendant. All you do is remove the loop portion of the pendant and use the remaining "rock" to create this gorgeous ring. Then, attach the stone's sterling silver setting to a band made of two strands of wire-threaded sterling silver beads. This sexy piece of jewelry is the perfect cocktail ring. Its added appeal is that it can be made in any size.

materials

- 1 faux tourmaline pendant, pink, 12mm wide x 16mm high x 8mm thick
- 30 round beads, laser finished sterling silver, 4mm dia.
- Silver wire, 22 gauge

tools

- Wire cutters
- Chain-nose pliers
- Ruler
- Round-nose pliers
- Metal file

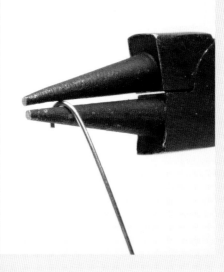

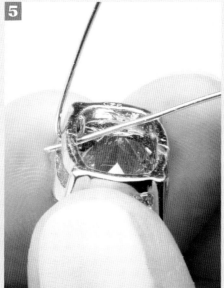

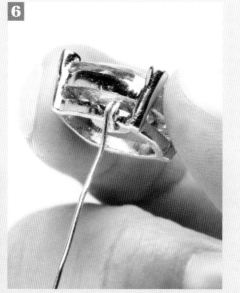

COSMOPOLITAN

1. Use wire cutters and chain-nose pliers to remove the loop from the pendant.

2. Use the wire cutters to cut two 6-in. lengths of wire.

3. Use the round-nose pliers to bend the end of one wire into a hook.

4. Hook the wire onto the side of the stone's setting.

5. Thread the end of the wire through the setting. Use the chain-nose pliers to hold the hooked end in place and, at the same time, pull the wire tight.

6. Repeat step 5 and wrap the wire around the side of the setting a second time.

materials

- 1 faux sapphire pendant, light blue, 1cm wide x 1cm high x 8mm thick
- 9 round beads, sterling silver, 2mm dia.
- 8 round beads, sterling silver, 4mm dia.
- Silver wire, 22 gauge

VARIATION: MANHATTAN

Fashioned from a square faux blue sapphire pendant in a sterling silver setting, "Manhattan" is the ideal cocktail ring, and can be made in any size. The stone is smaller than "Cosmopolitan" so only one band is made. To make the band, thread alternating small and large shiny sterling silver beads onto the wire, and attach it to the setting.

TIP

Just as inspiration was found in necklace pendants, look for other jewelry items with beautiful stones that have the potential to become incredible rings.

Little compares to the stunning impression that is made by a cocktail ring set with an oversized emerald-cut stone. For a canary diamond look-alike, consider using an emerald-cut citrine.

COSMOPOLITAN

7. String 15 beads onto the wire.

8. Wrap the wire around a finger to curve it, and adjust with the chain-nose pliers if necessary.

9. Thread the wire end through the other side of the setting.

10. Wrap the wire around the side of the setting.

11. Wrap the wire a second time. Use wire cutters to trim off the excess wire.

12. Use the metal file to smooth the cut ends.

13. Repeat steps 3–12 to make the second beaded band.

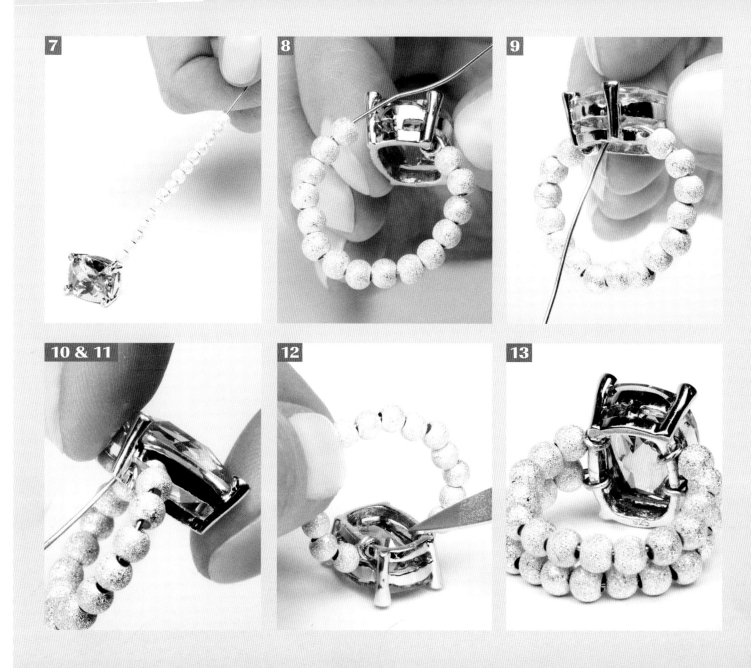

wrap star

materials
- 1 silver band with inlays of turquoise and mother of pearl
- 1 faceted turquoise stone, 14mm wide x 18mm high x 5mm thick
- Silver wire, 24 gauge

tools
- Ruler
- Wire cutters
- Chain-nose pliers
- Crystal cement
- Metal file

A sterling silver band with triangle inlays of turquoise and mother of pearl is a perfect backdrop for the faceted turquoise stone it showcases. Found in a thrift store, the band inspired the design. The stone is secured to the ring with a drop of glue and wire. The wire has two functions; it helps to secure the ring and is decorative, being cleverly wrapped around the stone to create triangle patterns similar to the band.

WRAP STAR

1. Use the wire cutters to cut an 8-in. length of wire.

2. Position the back of the stone vertically at the center of the wire. Have the wire approximately 4mm from the top of the stone.

3. Hold the wire on the back of the stone with the left hand. Wrap the end that extends at the right diagonally across the front of the stone to approximately 4mm from the bottom of the stone.

4. Wrap the same end behind the stone and to the right, approximately 4mm from the bottom of the stone.

5. Wrap the same end across the front of the stone diagonally, crossing the first wrap and ending approximately 4mm from the top of the stone.

6. Wrap the same end behind the stone.

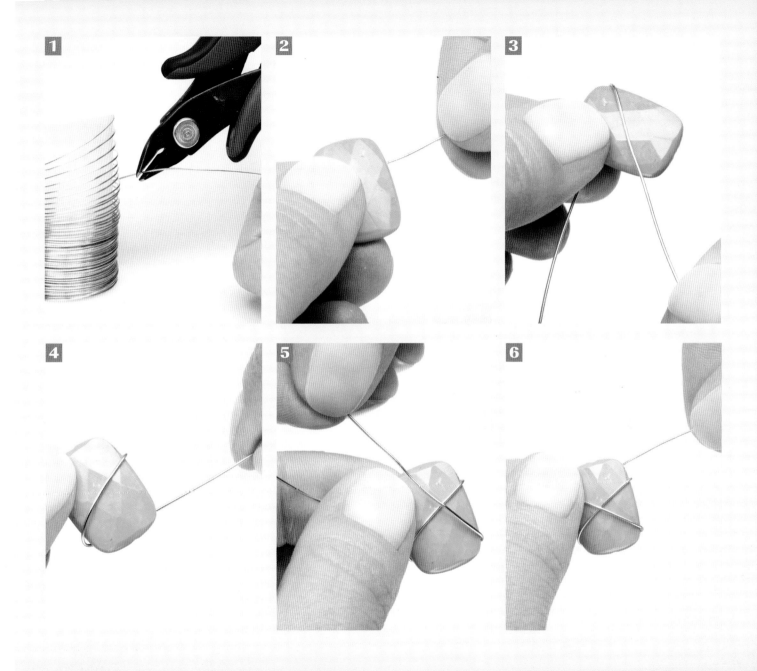

materials

- 1 ring form, silver, with a small disc for mounting stones
- 1 faceted frosted crystal nugget, 2cm wide x 2.5cm high x 1.5cm thick
- Silver wire, 24 gauge

Few things are more sought after than the proverbial "rock." Here "Wrap Star" and "Ice Cube" bring the "must-have" as close as your fingertips.

TIP

Wires are available in different shapes, allowing lots of possibilities when designing wrapped jewelry. Look for round, half-round, square, or triangle wires to provide inspiration.

VARIATION: ICE CUBE

A frosted white crystal nugget wrapped with multiple loops of wire, and mounted on a silver ring form becomes "Ice Cube." Glue the nugget to the ring form, and then encase it with wraps of wire from all directions. Use chain-nose pliers to help position the wire against the nugget. Twist the wire ends around the ring form's disc, trim off the excess wire, and smooth the cut ends with the file.

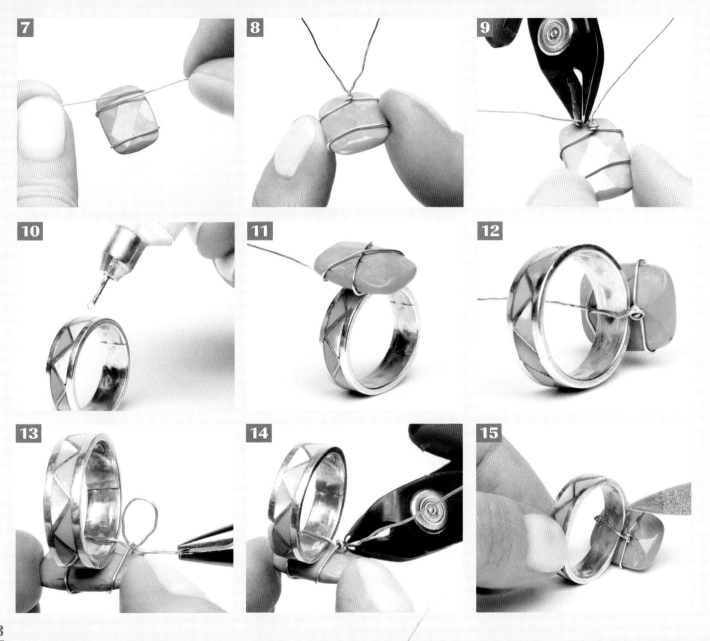

WRAP STAR

7. The back of the stone should look like the picture.

8. Twist the wire ends together.

9. Trim off the shorter end. Use the chain-nose pliers to bend the end against the twisted wire.

10. Apply a drop of glue to the top of the ring band.

11. Position the center back of the wrapped stone on the glue, and thread the remaining wire end through the center of the ring.

12. Thread the end under the wrap of wire at the back of the stone.

13. Use the chain-nose pliers to thread the end back under the wrap of wire, securing it.

14. Trim off the excess wire.

15. Use the file to smooth the wire's cut end, and any other cut ends.

cherry bomb

materials
- 1 ring form, in gold with 14 loops, 15mm wide x 18mm long
- 17 round dyed jade beads, red, 10mm dia.
- Transite

tools
- Ruler
- Wire cutters
- Crystal cement

techniques
- "How to Make a Single- and Double-Overhand Knot," see pg. 124

Highly polished red beads and as many beads as would fit are used to make this playful, oversized ring, "Cherry Bomb." The beads are made of dyed jade, and they are grouped in one large cluster on a golden ring form. The ring form has three rows of metal loops which make mounting the beads foolproof. Transite is used to attach the beads to the loops on the ring form.

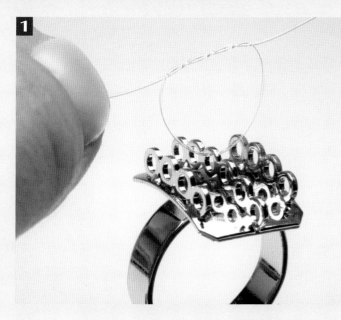

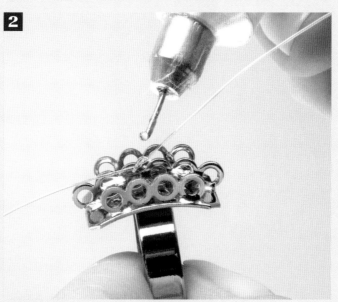

CHERRY BOMB

1. Use wire cutters to cut an 18-in. length of transite. Thread one end of the transite through the center loop on the ring form and tie a double-overhand knot.

2. Secure the knot with a drop of glue. Use wire cutters to trim off the short end of the transite.

3. String on one bead.

4. Thread the end of the transite through an adjacent loop. Adjust the bead so its holes are parallel with the ring form.

TIP

For different looks, try clustering smaller beads in a number of colors or faceted beads, which will catch the light.

materials

- 1 ring form, gold with 14 loops, 15mm wide x 18mm long
- 1 faux amethyst pendant, purple, 1.2cm square
- 50 (approximately) round beads, variegated orange, 8mm dia.
- 30 Austrian crystal bicones, orange, 3mm dia.
- 20 Austrian crystal bicones, light orange, 6mm dia.
- 1 package seed beads, clear, size 11
- 30 head pins, gold, 3cm long
- Wire, gold, 20 gauge

tools

- Chain-nose pliers
- Round-nose pliers

TIP
An alternative to attaching the beaded head pins directly to the loops on the ring form is to attach a group of head pins to a jump ring, and then attach the jump ring to the loop.

VARIATION: FIREWORKS

Sprays of orange beads seem to explode from a faux amethyst center in "Fireworks." This unique showpiece begins with the same ring form used for "Cherry Bomb." Wire the pendant to the center of the ring, threading the wire through the loops to secure it. Thread beads onto head pins, combining variegated orange beads, bicones in light and dark orange, and clear seed beads. Thread the smallest beads on the head pins first, and increase the bead size up the head pin. Follow the directions for "Paris Café" to create wrapped wire loops, and attach them to the loops on the ring form. Add head pins until the ring is full.

CHERRY BOMB

5. Tie another double overhand knot, and secure it with a drop of glue.

6. Repeat steps 3–5 to string on the remaining beads. Continue to adjust the beads to fill in holes and cover the sides of the ring form. Finish by tying a double-overhand knot, securing it with a drop of glue, and trimming off the end of transite.

This chunky ring is made using a versatile technique. Because the beads are attached to the loops on the ring form, one-at-a-time, you can thread on beads of different sizes, test-fitting each new bead as you work.

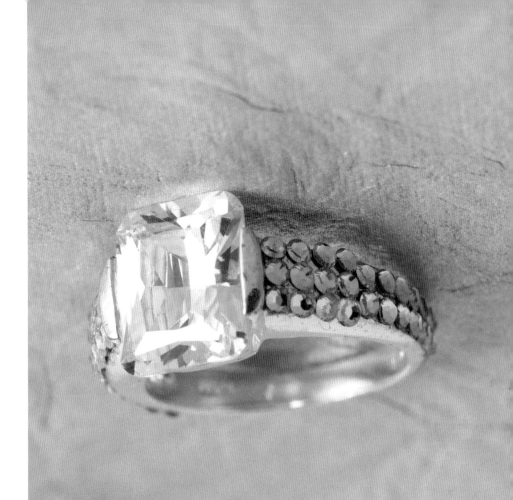

on the rocks

T his sterling silver band with a large square-cut cubic zirconia was a great find at a local thrift store. The silver band was wide enough to accommodate rows of small crystal rhinestones that mimic a channel setting on a diamond ring. The only technique required to make this stunner is gluing (and the patience to find the rhinestones that get away). This project is easy and fun because the glitzy and glamorous knock-off, "On The Rocks," makes up in practically no time.

materials
- 1 ring with wide band (2mm to 6mm wide), sterling silver, set with an emerald-cut cubic zirconia
- 1 package (200 pcs.) Swarovski crystal rhinestones, crystal, size SS-5, 2mm dia.

tools
- Five-minute two-part epoxy
- Scrap cardboard
- Toothpicks
- Tweezers

ON THE ROCKS

1. Mix the two-part epoxy on scrap cardboard following the manufacturer's directions. Dip a toothpick into the glue and apply the glue to the back of a rhinestone.

2. Pick up the rhinestone with the tweezers and position it on the ring's band.

TIP
After trying a number of glues, such as crystal cement and cyanoacrylate gel, I found that epoxy works best. It is worth the extra effort required to ensure that the rhinestones are permanently adhered.

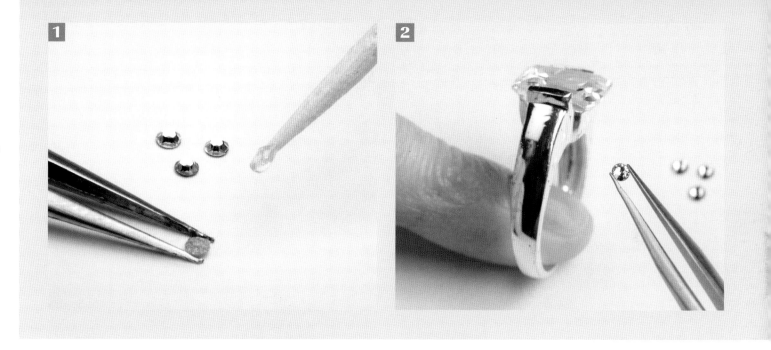

There is much to be said for the unabashed proportions of "On the Rocks." An oversized cubic zirconia leaves no doubt that this is a ring about getting noticed. The rhinestones raise the amps on sparkle and shine.

VARIATION: TRIO

A dazzling sterling silver ring with three bands, "Trio" features rhinestones in shades of pink. The outside bands have deep-pink rhinestones, contrasting with the light-pink center band. Trio is easy to make, requiring only some gluing. Follow the directions for "On The Rocks," positioning the rhinestones in a single row along each band.

This ring, "Trio," is named for the three delicate silver bands that are decorated with pink rhinestones. For a ring that matches "On the Rocks," use rhinestones in crystal instead.

TIP
When choosing a ring, make sure the band is wide enough to accommodate the rhinestones. Be aware that some rhinestones may only be available in certain sizes and colors.

materials
- 1 ring with three bands, sterling silver, 2.5mm wide
- 1 package (200 pcs.) Swarovski crystal rhinestones, light pink, size SS-7, 2.2mm dia.
- 1 package (200 pcs.) Swarovski crystal rhinestones, pink, size SS-7, 2.2mm dia.

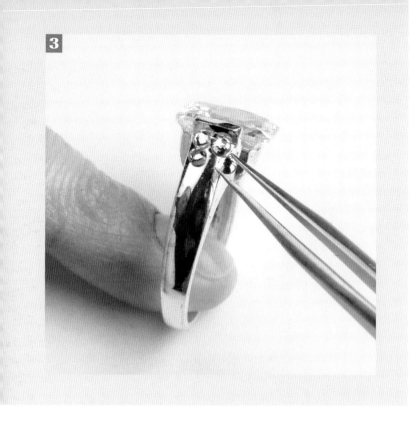

3

ON THE ROCKS

3. Continue to apply glue to the rhinestones, and position them in rows along the ring's band. Apply rhinestones to the entire band and to the sides of the ring, if desired.

TIP
Epoxy does not dry instantly, which is great because it allows a bit of time to reposition the rhinestones, if necessary. However, it is best to have all your beads laid out before you begin gluing them.

Look for chunky costume jewelry that you can enhance with rhinestones. For a subtle look, add citrine-colored rhinestones to rings and pendants in gold tone to jazz them up.

3

in bloom

Several small, white iridescent beads are the center of the flower, and briolettes in hot pink and pale blue form the petals of this floral ring. The ring form has two parts. The band has a platform with prongs that holds a removable beading disc. The beading disc is covered with holes so that the beads can be "sewn" on. When beading is complete, the disc is placed back onto the pronged platform and secured by closing the prongs with pliers.

materials

- 1 two-part ring form, silver with removable beading disc, 2cm dia.
- 7 faceted iridescent round beads, white, 5mm dia.
- 5 faceted dyed jade briolettes, pink, top-drilled, 14mm wide x 16mm long x 4mm thick
- 5 faceted opaque quartz briolettes, blue, top-drilled, 6mm dia. x 10mm thick
- Transite

tools

- Ruler
- Wire cutters
- Crystal cement
- Chain-nose pliers

techniques

- "How to Make a Single- and Double-Overhand Knot," see pg. 124

1

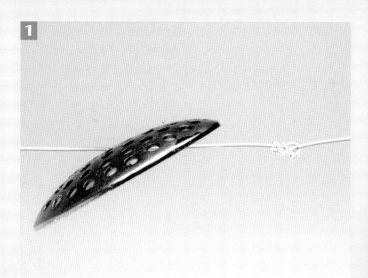

2

3

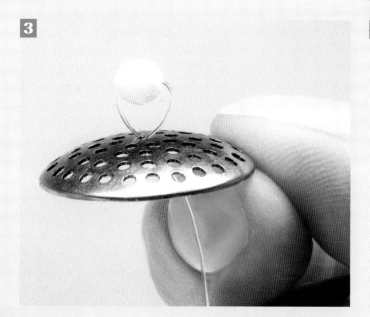

4

IN BLOOM

1. Use wire cutters to cut a 12-in. length of transite beading cord. Make a double-overhand knot at one end of the transite. Secure the knot with a drop of glue. Thread the other end through the center back of the beading disc. Pull the transite so that the knot is tight against the disc.

2. String the center white bead onto the transite at the front of the disc.

3. Thread the transite through an adjacent hole in the disc, and pull it tight so the bead rests against the disc. Adjust the bead so its holes are parallel with the disc.

4. Thread on the remaining six white beads, spaced around the center bead, to complete the flower center.

materials

- 1 ring form, silver, with attached concave beading disc, 1.5cm dia.
- 1 oval turquoise bead, 2.5cm wide x 3cm long x 1.5cm thick
- Transite

TIP

To secure the stone with glue after it has been attached with transite, place the ring face down. Apply small drops of glue to the beading-disc holes. The glue will seep under the disc, securing the stone.

VARIATION: ROCK 'N' BLUES

The ring form used for "Rock 'N' Blues" differs slightly from "In Bloom," yet the same technique is used to secure this large turquoise bead to its beading disc. The disc on this ring is attached to the band and is concave to accommodate a large bead. Follow steps 2–3, threading the transite through the holes on the edge of the disc. Knot the end at the back, and apply glue to the knot. Place the ring face down, and apply small drops of glue to the disc holes. The glue will seep under the disc, securing the bead.

In "Rock 'N' Blues," a single, polished turquoise bead, whose intricate surface has refined tracery, is given center stage in a simple but sophisticated ring.

IN BLOOM

5. Follow steps 2–3, and thread on the five blue briolettes, evenly spaced around the disc.

6. Follow steps 2–3, and thread on the five pink briolettes, each placed between a blue briolette. Tie a double-overhand knot in the transite, flush against the back of the disc, and secure it with a drop of glue. Trim the transite ends to ⅛ in.

7. Position the beading disc on the ring platform.

8. Use the chain-nose pliers to close the prongs around the ring platform, securing the beading disc.

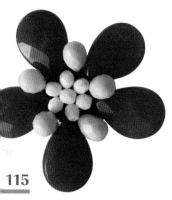

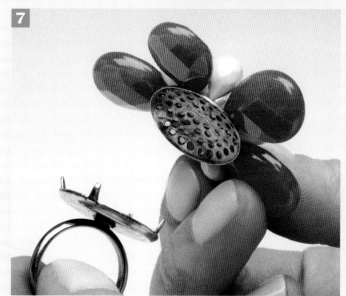

BEADING BASICS

I n this section, you will find an overview

of the fundamental types of beads,

tools, strands, and findings, together with

more in-depth information for several of

the most commonly used jewelry-making

techniques. You will find that the more

familiar you are with the basics, the more

confident, skilled, and imaginative you will

become.

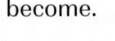

MATERIALS

beads

There is an infinite number of bead shapes available—rondelle, faceted, briolette, square, disc, tube, and chips being among the most common. Every shape of bead comes in a wide variey of materials and sizes.

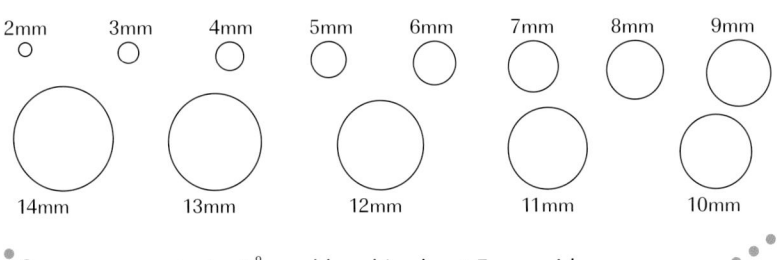

measurements

Beads are commonly measured in millimeters (mm). Generally, the higher the number, the larger the bead. The exception to this is seed beads, whose size is indicated by numbers. The higher the number, the smaller the bead.

2mm   3mm   4mm   5mm   6mm   7mm   8mm   9mm

14mm   13mm   12mm   11mm   10mm

A size 5° seed bead is about 5mm wide;
a size 11 is about 2mm wide.

TOOLS

The number of tools needed to accomplish most of the basic beading techniques is surprisingly small. The essential tools pictured here can equip you to make all the projects in "The Collection."

emery cloth

beading needles

epoxy

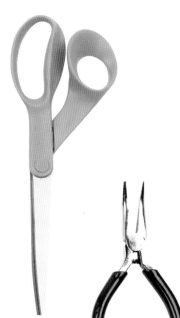

crystal cement

tweezers

metal nail file

cyanoacrylate (instant glue) gel

round-nose pliers

small chain-nose pliers

large chain-nose pliers

scissors

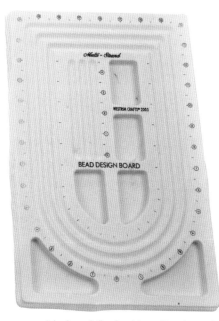

molded and flocked beading board

wire snips

memory wire cutters

crimping pliers

bent-nose pliers

STRANDS

The material upon which particular beads are strung is determined by the weight and the aesthetic effect desired. Traditionally, the heavier the bead, the stronger the strand material.

gold wire

silver wire

nylon-coated stainless-steel beading wire

memory wire

nylon beading thread

transite

monofilament

MONOFILAMENT FISHING LINE
HIGH KNOT STRENGTH
ABRASION RESISTANT
30 LB | 180 YD

NYLON COATED
#44X7
LENGTH 100M
STAINLESS STEEL WIRE

gold chain

FINDINGS

Findings can be described as those jewelry-making elements, usually made of metal, that connect different components in a piece of jewelry.

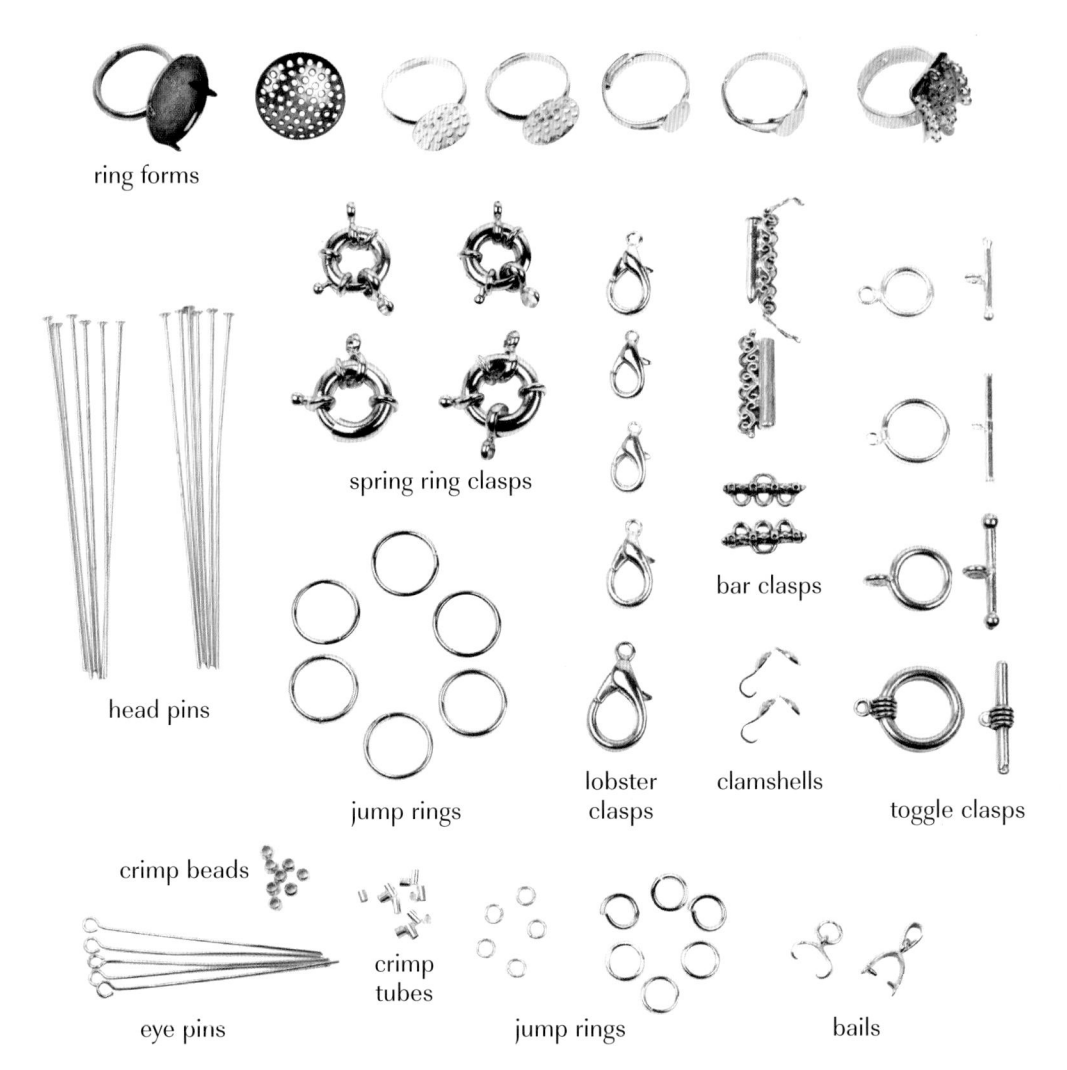

ring forms

spring ring clasps

bar clasps

head pins

jump rings

lobster clasps

clamshells

toggle clasps

crimp beads

eye pins

crimp tubes

jump rings

bails

TECHNIQUES

how to use a crimp tube

Crimp tubes are used together with crimping pliers to secure strand material to findings, like jump rings and clasps.

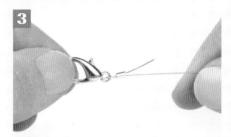

1. Thread a crimp tube and a lobster clasp onto the beading wire.

2. Thread the end of the short wire through the crimp tube.

3. Hold the wires, and slide the crimp tube against the base of the clasp.

5. Place the crimp tube in the front portion of the crimping pliers, and press down, folding the crimp tube in half.

4. Place the crimp tube in the back crescent portion of the crimping pliers, and press down.

Detail: The crimp tube should have one wire in each section of the cutoff tube.

Detail: The completed crimp tube should look like this when finished.

TIP

A crimp bead is smaller than a crimp tube. To affix, follow steps 1 through 6 above.

Crimp tubes are sized 1–4 according to their diameters. Choose a crimp tube through which the strand(s) snugly pass. A crimp tube that is too large can slip off.

how to make a wrapped wire loop

1. Insert the head pin through one disc.

2. Then thread on one crystal bead and a second disc.

3. Use the chain-nose pliers to grasp the head pin ⅛ in. above the top bead. Hold the bead with the other hand, and turn the pliers away from you to bend the head pin stem at a 90-degree angle.

4. Grasp the head pin ⅛ in. from the bend using the round-nose pliers. Rotate the pliers toward the bend, and use your fingers to bend the head pin around the jaw of the pliers.

5. Cross the wire in front of the stem to make a loop.

6. Grasp the loop with the bent-nose pliers, and use the chain-nose pliers to wrap the head pin around the stem, moving from the loop down toward the first bead.

7. Use the wire cutters to trim away any excess wire. Use an emery cloth to smooth the wire end.

8. Use the chain-nose pliers to squeeze the cut end of wire flush against the stem.

Example of a finished bead with a wrapped wire loop

how to use a clamshell

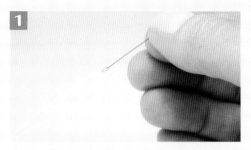
1

2

3

1. Double-thread a beading needle with beading thread. Double-knot the end.

2. Insert the needle through the hole in the clamshell from the inside.

3. Pull the thread through the clamshell until the knot is about 1 in. away from the clamshell. Use scissors to trim loose threads around the knot.

4

5

4. Place a drop of glue on the knot to secure it.

5. Pull the knot into the clamshell. Close the clamshell using the chain-nose pliers. Use the needle at the opposite end to string on beads.

how to attach a clamshell

1

2

3

1. Use the pliers to grasp the open halves of the clamshell. Slowly squeeze the halves together.

2. Hang a jump ring on the clamshell's hook. Grasp the front of the hook using the chain-nose pliers.

3. Roll the pliers toward you to close the hook around the jump ring.

HOW NOT TO CLOSE A CLAMSHELL

When attaching a clamshell to a jump ring or to a clasp, follow the directions above. Do NOT place the entire clamshell in the jaws of the chain-nose pliers and squeeze. The pliers will flatten the shell-shape bottom of the clamshell.

how to use a clamshell to cover a crimp bead*

1

2

3

4

1. Insert the end of the strand into the clamshell, followed by a crimp bead. Thread the end through one hole on the bar clasp, and back through the crimp bead. Use the crescent-shaped portion of the crimping pliers to secure the crimp bead.

2. Slide the clamshell along the strand until the crimp bead is inside the clamshell and the hook on the clamshell is threaded through the hole in the bar clasp.

3. Use the chain-nose pliers to close the clamshell around the crimp bead.

4. Hang the hook on the clamshell over the strand. Use pliers to grasp the hook, and roll it toward you to secure the clamshell and hide the strand.

*The technique detailed here can be used to cover a crimp tube.

how to open and close a jump ring

1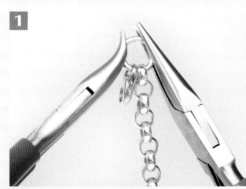

1. Use chain-nose and bent-nose pliers to grasp the jump ring on opposite sides, as shown.

2

2. Rotate your wrists so that one hand moves toward you while the other moves away.

creating a knotted necklace

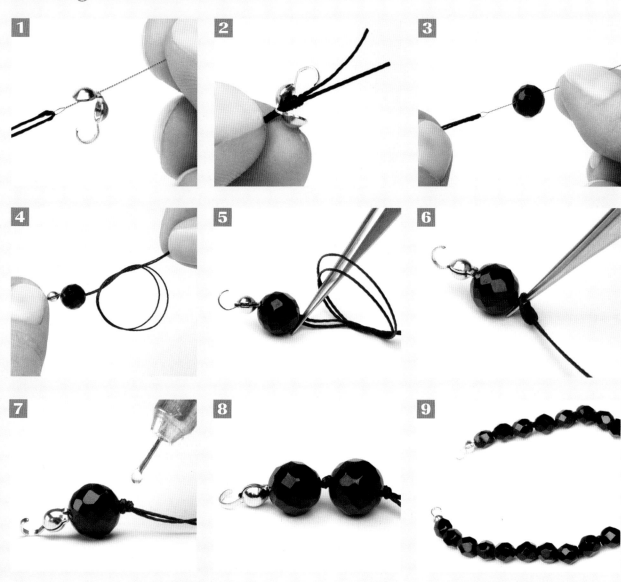

Follow these simple steps when making a knotted necklace. Be sure to add at least 2–3 inches extra to your stringing material measurement to allow for the knots. For a bracelet, only 1–2 inches is necessary.

1. Use a double-threaded beading needle with a knotted end to thread on one clamshell, sliding it down to the knot.

2. Apply a drop of crystal cement to the knot; let it dry. Pull the knot into the clamshell. Trim off excess threads, and use chain-nose pliers to close the clamshell.

3. Thread the needle through one bead, and slide it to the end with the clamshell.

4. Tie a single-overhand knot, but do not pull it tight.

5. While holding the threads with one hand, use the other hand to place the tips of the tweezers through the knot and against the bead.

6. While holding the tweezers, pull the threads to tighten the knot flush against the bead.

7. Place the smallest drop of glue possible on the knot. Be sure not to get any glue on the bead.

8. Repeat steps 5–8 to make the knot after the second bead.

9. When finished, thread the needle through the remaining clamshell. Tie a double-overhand knot into the clamshell, and repeat step 3. The strand is complete and can be attached to an end bar, jump ring, etc.

how to make a single- and a double-overhand knot

1

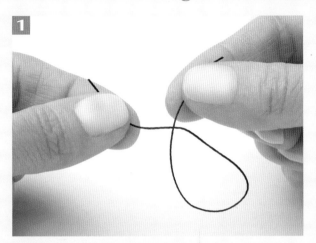

1. To make a single-overhand knot, bring the ends of the thread together, crossing the right thread over the left.

2

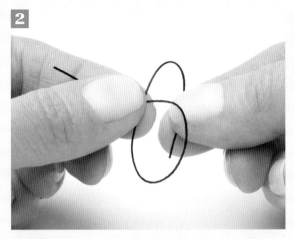

2. Bring the right thread around the loop to the back, and thread it into the center of the loop.

3

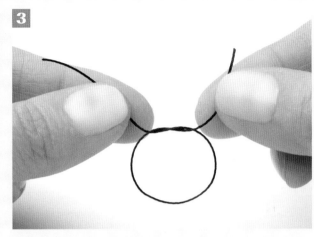

3. Pull the ends of the thread to make a single overhand knot.

4

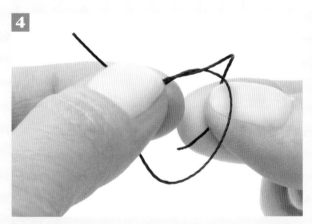

4. To make a double-overhand knot, repeat step 2.

5

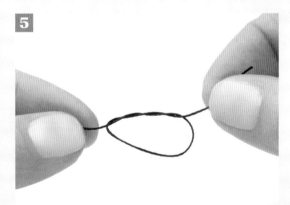

5. Then pull the ends of the threads to secure the knot in place.

TIP
Double-overhand knots are well suited to bracelets and necklaces made from pearls. The knots will keep the pearls from sliding off a broken strand.

sources and resources

Bazaar Star Beadery
216 East Ridgewood Ave.
Ridgewood, NJ 07450
(201) 444-5144
www.bazaarstarbeadery.com
Loose and strung beads;
crenulated brass beads

Fire Mountain Gems and Beads
One Fire Mountain Way
Grants Pass, OR 97526
(800) 423-2319
www.firemountaingems.com
Beads and findings

Fun 2 Bead
1028 Sixth Ave.
New York, NY 10018
(212) 302-3488
www.fun2bead.com
Loose and strung beads,
findings

Genuine Ten Ten
1010 Sixth Ave.
New York, NY 10018
(212) 221-1173
Loose and strung beads,
findings

Kate's Paperie
1282 Third Ave.
New York, NY 10021
(212) 396-3670
(800) 809-9880
www.katespaperie.com
Handmade papers and gift
wraps (Background papers for
all photographs)

M&J Trimming
1008 Sixth Ave.
New York, NY 10018
212.204.9595
(800) 965-8746
www.mjtrim.com
Ribbons, Sworovski crystal
rhinestones, beads, belt buckles

Michael's Stores, Inc.
8000 Bent Branch Dr.
Irving, TX 75063
(800) 642-4235
www.michaels.com
National craft supply store with
comprehensive beading section

New York Beads
1026 Sixth Ave.
New York, NY 10018

(212) 382-2994
Loose and strung beads

Toho Shoji
990 Sixth Ave.
New York, NY 10018
(212) 868-7466
www.tohoshojiny.com
Beads, findings, and chains

Wonder Sources, Inc.
48 W. 38th St.
Ground Floor
New York, NY 10018
(212) 563-4990
www.wondersources.com
Loose and strung beads

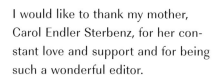

acknowledgments

I would like to thank my mother, Carol Endler Sterbenz, for her constant love and support and for being such a wonderful editor.

I would also like to thank the entire team at Creative Homeowner for all their hard work.

Thank you to my incredibly brilliant and talented photographers: Steven Mays, Dennis Johnson, and Damian Sandone.

Thank you to M&J Trimming and Kate's Paperie for their generous contributions. A special thanks to Michelle Beshaw and Aahzion Fonrose from the Third Avenue Kate's Paperie store for their indispensable and expert help.

Big thanks to the Johnson Family: Dennis, Laura, and little Isabel, for their kindness and hospitality.

And finally, thank you to Frank Santopadre, who shows me every day how good my life can be.

index

If you like **Bead Style** take a look at **Knit Style** and **Jeans Style**

Knit Style is a collection of 25 chic and sexy accessories for every occasion, each original item knitted in today's most popular yarns, like fun fur, chenille, and chunky. It has everything you need to add gorgeous items to your wardrobe.

- Over 125 full-color photographs
- For beginner and veteran knitter alike
- Clear and concise step-by-step patterns and professional knitting tips
- An easel-back, spiral-bound book that allows "hands-free" access to information

Knit Style
ISBN: 1-58011-305-2
UPC: 0-78585-11305-7
CH Book # 265142
128 pages, 7¾" x 10⅞"
$19.95 US / $24.95 CAN

Jean Style shows you fast and fabulous ways to customize your jeans using embellishments of every kind.

- 34 great-looking jeans made with amazing creative techniques
- Professional secrets for transforming last-season's jeans into the latest styles
- Comprehensive sections like "Decorating Basics" and "Sources and Resources"
- An easel-back, spiral-bound book that allows "hands-free" access to the information on each page

Jean Style
ISBN: 1-58011-320-6
UPC: 0-78585-11320-0
CH Book # 265154
128 pages, 7¾" x 10⅞"
$19.95 US / $24.95 CAN

You might also like these other titles in our Home Arts series

The Decorated Bag
ISBN: 1-58011-296-X
UPC: 0-78585-11296-8
CH Book # 265138
144 pages, 8½" x 9½"
$19.95 US / $24.95 CAN

Glamorous Beaded Jewelry
ISBN: 1-58011-295-1
UPC: 0-78585-11295-1
CH Book # 265133
144 pages, 8½" x 9½"
$19.95 US / $24.95 CAN

Look for these and other fine **Creative Homeowner** books wherever books are sold.
For more information and to order direct, go to **www.creativehomeowner.com**